AMERICA CELEBRATES

IDEALS PUBLICATIONS INCORPORATED

NASHVILLE, TENNESSEE

Acknowledgments

LOVE, AND ALL THAT! from *HEADFIRST IN THE PICKLE BARREL* by John Rolfe Burroughs, copyright © 1963 by John Rolfe Burroughs. Published by William Morrow & Company. Used with permission. A MOTHER'S LOVE by Grace Noll Crowell, reprinted with permission of the author's estate. A FATHER'S JOB from *LIFE'S HIGHWAY* by Edgar A. Guest, copyright © 1933 by The Reilly & Lee Co., reprinted with permission of the author's estate. LABOR DAY, MEMORIAL DAY, and TO HER by Edgar A. Guest, reprinted with permission of the author's estate. MOTHER'S DAY and THE OLD-FASHIONED CHRISTMAS EVE from *LOVE AND LAUGHTER* by Marjorie Holmes, copyright © 1967 by Marjorie Holmes Mighell. Used by permission of the author and Doubleday, a division of Bantam Doubleday Dell Publishing Group, Inc. SCHOOL from *LAKE WOBEGON DAYS* by Garrison Keillor, copyright © 1985 by Garrison Keillor. Used by permission of Viking Penguin, a division of Penguin Books USA Inc. THE CRUNCH OF GRAVEL from *MY FATHER'S HOUSE* by Philip B. Kunhardt, Jr., copyright © 1958, 1967, 1970 by Philip B. Kunhardt, Jr. Published by Random House. Used with permission. CHRISTMAS, AND I REMEMBER and LILACS FOR MEMORIAL DAY from *NEW ENGLAND HERITAGE AND OTHER POEMS* by Rose Koralewsky, copyright © 1949 by Bruce Humphries, Inc. Reprinted with permission of Branden Publishing Company, Boston. HE IS RISEN! by Edgar Daniel Kramer, reprinted with permission of the author's estate. EASTER AT THE WHITE HOUSE from *EASTER THE WORLD OVER* by Priscilla S. Lord and Daniel J. Foley. Copyright © 1971. Reprinted with the permission of the publisher, Chilton Book Company, Radnor, Pennsylvania. Excerpts from SEPTEMBER and NOVEMBER from *STILL COVE JOURNAL* by Gladys Taber, copyright © 1975, 1976 by Gladys Taber. All rights reserved. Reprinted by permission of Brandt & Brandt Literary Agents, Inc. Our sincere thanks to the following authors whom we were unable to contact: Carrie M. Adamson for MY MOTHER'S HANDS; Sylvia Trent Auxier for PLEA TO SEPTEMBER from *LOVE-VINE*, copyright © 1953 by Sylvia Trent Auxier; Horatio Nelson Powers for THE NEW YEAR; and Violet Alleyn Storey for THE FATHER.

Chapter openings are details of original Norman Rockwell illustrations, used with permission of the Norman Rockwell Family Trust, copyright © 1996 the Norman Rockwell Family Trust.

Editor, Michelle Prater Burke; Designer, Anne Lesemann

Printed and bound in the U.S.A.

ISBN 0-8249-4071-7

Film separations by WebTech Inc.
Printed by RR Donnelley & Sons

CONTENTS

New Year's Day

A Time for

Friends and

Resolutions

"The good old year is with the past,
Oh, be the new as kind!"

–WILLIAM CULLEN BRYANT

As one of the only holidays celebrated worldwide by people of all beliefs, New Year's Day is filled with a wealth of traditions. Centuries ago, people around the globe began celebrating the beginning of a new year with noisemaking (to scare out the old year), hearty food (to symbolize prosperity in the upcoming year), reunions with friends and family (complete with small gifts to ensure good luck), and quiet contemplation (to pray for a year of blessings). These ancient traditions have grown into the popular American holiday of today.

New Year's Day is probably the oldest holiday still celebrated and has been anticipated for years as a time of new beginnings. It is no surprise, then, that the holiday has often been observed with festivals and feasts. As early as 2600 B.C., the Babylonians celebrated the first day of their calendar year with a great eleven-day festival. Centuries later, the people of Scotland spent the first evening of the year at special church services; they then went "first-footing," which involved calling on friends from midnight to one o'clock A.M. The night was filled with wishes of good health for the new year.

Similar traditions of visiting others on New Year's Day were popular throughout Europe and were brought to America by the new settlers. President George Washington began the pleasant practice of hosting an open house for the general public, a New Year's tradition that continued until this century. During these early years of our country, the socially astute spent the day traveling from one gala event to another. These parties were filled with much merriment and food unlike anything offered throughout the year, and the partygoers often continued the festivities until dawn.

The joyous, raucous feeling of New Year's (along with a need to attract tourists) led the townspeople of Pasadena, California, to plan a parade of flower-decorated horse and buggies and public games to celebrate New Year's Day in 1890. After the parade, young men competed in foot races, tugs of war, jousts, and a game called the "tourney of rings." It was this game, coupled with the exquisite floral displays, that prompted the title "The Tournament of Roses," which has been a favorite New Year's tradition in America for the past one hundred years.

For many people, however, the first day of the year has always remained a time for reflection. New Year's Day is often spent at religious services and in quiet thought, considering the blessings of the past year and making resolutions for the year ahead.

Centuries-old traditions and rich cultural influences have made New Year's Day a holiday that all Americans can enjoy. Whether celebrated with festive reunions among friends and family or solemn contemplation, the first day of the year is a joyful time when the ancient cry of "Happy New Year!" can be heard nationwide, welcoming a new year full of opportunity.

The Land of Beginning Again

LOUISA FLETCHER

I wish that there were some wonderful place
Called the Land of Beginning Again
Where all our mistakes and all our
    heartaches
And all of our poor selfish grief
Could be dropped like a shabby old coat at
    the door
And never be put on again.

I wish we could come on it all unaware,
Like the hunter who finds a lost trail;
And I wish that the one whom our blindness
    had done
The greatest injustice of all
Could be at the gates like an old friend who
    waits
For the comrade he's gladdest to hail.

We would find all the things we intended
    to do
But forgot, and remembered too late,
Little praises unspoken, little promises
    broken,
And all of the thousand and one
Little duties neglected that might have
    perfected
The day for one less fortunate.

It wouldn't be possible not to be kind
In the Land of Beginning Again;
And the ones we misjudged and the ones
    whom we grudged
Their moments of victory here
Would find in the grasp of our loving
    handclasp
More than penitent lips could explain.

For what had been hardest we'd know had
    been best,
And what had seemed loss would be gain;
For there isn't a sting that will not take wing
When we've faced it and laughed it away;
And I think that the laughter is most what
    we're after
In the Land of Beginning Again.

So I wish that there were some wonderful
    place
Called the Land of Beginning Again
Where all our mistakes and all our
    heartaches
And all of our poor selfish grief
Could be dropped like a shabby old coat at
    the door
And never be put on again.

New Year's Open House

PAMELA KENNEDY

I love New Year's Day. It heralds the beginning of a fresh year full of possibilities and devoid of failures. From the vantage point of January first, three hundred and sixty-five brand new days wait like empty pages ready to be filled. I stand with my back to the past and my face to the future, eager for any challenge life throws my way. Well, almost any challenge.

Last New Year's Day I actually stood with my back to the kitchen door and my face toward the broiler as I anxiously watched my stuffed mushrooms become the first dark blot on the opening page of the new year. It all happened because my husband decided sometime in early December that we should have a New Year's Open House and invite some friends and business associates. Filled with pre-Christmas charity, I agreed. By December 26, however, I had second thoughts. When New Year's Day dawned, I wanted to relish it restfully, not prepare relishes fretfully.

"It will be easy," my husband assured me. "It's not like you have to fix a big meal. Just throw together some finger food. People will come and graze for a couple of hours. It will be fun; you'll see."

Let me mention here that this advice comes from a man whose idea of entertaining is lighting the candles before the guests are seated and who believes a gourmet meal should include a cheeseburger. I was sure our visitors would expect more than a casual graze. And who says finger food is easy anyway? I'd rather put together a complete meal than assemble a variety of appetizers. In my book, appetizers are much ado about nothing. I spend days shopping for obscure food found only in specialty shops and labor for hours arranging pimiento slices, hearts of palm, and capers to look like birds of paradise. Then they vanish in one bite.

With the invitations already delivered, I decided my complaints would be useless. Reluctantly, I hauled out my cookbooks and leafed through them looking for interesting hors d'oeuvres that appeared easy as well as edible.

After selecting a variety of recipes, I spent a few days accumulating the required ingredients. Then on December 30, I set up an assembly line, determined to prepare as much as I could ahead of time. With adequate organization, I believed I could still salvage some time on New Year's Day for reflection and contemplation.

By New Year's Eve, the refrigerator was filled with plastic-encased packages bearing threatening notes: "Don't even think about eating this." "Party food. Beware!" (You have to do this when you have hungry teen-agers in the house.)

When New Year's Day dawned, I realized the futility of my plan to contemplate the brave new year waiting at my door. In a few hours, fifty or sixty hungry folks would be marching through that door expecting to be fed. It was time for action. I enlisted all available family members to arrange furniture, set up the serving tables, and keep the cat out of the clam dip.

By 2:00 P.M., when our guests started arriving, we had an impressive variety of appetizers on display; and I admitted this open house idea might be okay after all. The hum of conversations punctuated with laughter filled the house, and our visitors grazed cheerfully. Smiling with parental pride, I watched our teen-age son cruise around the room carrying a tray of crab puffs. I thought he was utterly charming as he engaged our guests in friendly banter until I overheard his exchange with a neighbor.

"Please take a few more, Mr. Johnson. If I don't get rid of these, I'm gonna be stuck eating them for a week!" I pulled him aside for a quick refresher in open house etiquette, then turned him loose again with a platter of asparagus rolls and a stern warning against editorializing.

Rushing back to the kitchen to check on the stuffed mushrooms, I arrived just as their edges began to char, sending acrid fumes curling ominously toward the smoke alarm. In a panic, I grabbed the broiler pan and yanked it out of the oven, launching a dozen or so mushrooms in the process. A quick glance toward the kitchen door revealed that my near-disaster was undiscovered, and in a flash I gathered up my wayward mushroom caps. Despite my best efforts to arrange them attractively on a platter, the presentation lacked appeal. Determined to salvage what I could, I scraped off the burned stuffing and covered the blackened edges with slices of provolone cheese. A few seconds in the microwave, and my creations were ready.

The first person to bite into a "mushroom cheese surprise" was a neighbor renowned for her entertaining skills. I could tell by her puzzled expression that the flavor baffled her well-trained taste buds. Believing that the best defense is a good offense, I whispered, "Don't you just love this exotic nouvelle cuisine: *char du jour*?" Handing her a cup of punch, I smiled graciously and quickly excused myself.

Peeking into the family room, I found most of the male guests hunkering in front of the television, munching pretzels, and analyzing the pass defenses of various college football teams.

In the living room, the women ate quiche with pesto sauce and discussed the merits of the new music teacher at the junior high school. Feelings were running high regarding his innovative approach to integrating classical and contemporary music; he called it "Rock-a-Bach."

"Utterly ridiculous," offered one guest, a member of the local chamber music group.

"How will children ever appreciate the musical legacy of the masters with that kind of garbage being taught as music?"

"Well they certainly won't get it if they're bored to death like we were in music appreciation class," retorted the mother of a teen-ager. "Why do some people always resist new ideas?"

I sensed trouble as the first woman, flushed with indignation, very pointedly set down her plate and opened her mouth to reply.

"Asparagus rolls anyone? Get 'em while they're hot!" What my irrepressible son lacked in decorum, he made up for in timing; and I almost kissed him. His interruption silenced the music critics, and the moment of confrontation passed.

The afternoon proceeded without further incident; and after the last guest departed, my husband and I relaxed on the couch. As we munched on leftovers, the cat strolled by with a satisfied gleam in her eye and an unmistakable trace of clam dip on her whiskers.

"Now didn't you think that was fun?" asked my husband, spreading cheese on a cracker. "I sure had a great time."

I recalled the hours of preparation and looked at all the dirty plates, used napkins, and half-filled glasses. "Part of it was fun," I admitted. "But New Year's Day is over, and I haven't even had time to think about the year ahead."

He appraised me thoughtfully, then pointed toward the front door with a celery stick. "The year ahead," he began philosophically, "stretches before you like an unwritten book. Opportunity stands at the door. Your back is to the past, your face is toward the future. . . ."

He ducked as I swung at him with a decorative pillow.

"Hold everything!" our son interrupted, sweeping into the room with a tray of uneaten appetizers. "How about a few asparagus rolls? Or maybe a crab puff? We have some of these great burnt mushroom things left. It's a long, hard journey to the future you know; I'd sure hate for you to start off on an empty stomach!"

New Year's Reverie

MARY E. LINTON

Tonight I would be quiet for a while,
No raucous horns, no screeching jubilee,
Only by firelight now review the file
Of hoarded treasure held in memory.
All of the rich year's golden store, the brief,
Bright moments and the deeper tones of pain
Stand out against the embers in relief.
Hold close the year that will not come again.
Then on the living ashes still aglow,
Another log, a leaping tongue of flame,
And all the unknown way that we must go
Is warmed and lighted as the way we came.
Builders of dreams, we hold these moments dear.
Magic, enchanting—this might be the year!

Hearty Chicken and Noodles

In a heavy pot, place a cut-up, 2½- to 3-pound chicken; cover with water and bring to a boil. Skim off foam and discard. Add 2 large, quartered yellow onions; 2 large, sliced carrots; 4 sliced ribs celery; 2 cloves garlic; 2 bay leaves; 2 teaspoons thyme; 2 teaspoons salt; and pepper to taste. Reduce heat; simmer 4 to 5 hours.

In a large bowl, combine 1 beaten egg, 2 tablespoons milk, and ½ teaspoon salt. Stir in 1 cup flour; dough will be stiff. Cover and let rest 10 minutes. Divide dough in half. On a floured surface, roll dough into a 16-by-12-inch rectangle. Let rest 20 minutes. Roll up loosely; cut into ¼-inch-thick slices. Unroll; dry on wire rack or flat, floured surface 2 hours.

Remove chicken from broth. Strain broth; return to pot or chill until fat rises to surface and can be removed. Discard skin and bones; cut up meat and set aside. Bring broth to a boil; add noodles. Cover; simmer 10 minutes. Add chicken. In a jar with a lid, combine ½ cup milk and ½ cup flour. Shake to mix thoroughly. Slowly add milk mixture to broth, stirring constantly. Add additional milk, if needed, to desired consistency. Serve hot. Makes approximately 12 servings.

The New Year

HORATIO NELSON POWERS

A flower unblown, a book unread,
A tree with fruit unharvested,
A path untrod, a house whose rooms
Lack yet the heart's divine perfumes,
A landscape whose wide border lies
In silent shade neath silent skies,
A treasure with its gifts concealed—
This is the year that for you waits
Beyond tomorrow's mystic gates.

A Passing Shadow

E. COLE INGLE

Only the moon beyond the windowsill,
Only the wind upon a winter hill
Follow the shadow of the dying year,
Watching it fade and swiftly disappear.
Only the pensive share the rendezvous
She keeps with time, her spirit passing through
Into remembered ways. Erased from earth,
Only the heart retains her golden worth.

Alexander's Ragtime Band

WORDS AND MUSIC
BY IRVING BERLIN

Come on and hear, come on and hear Al-ex-an-der's rag-time band; Come on and hear, come on and hear, it's the best band in the land. They can play a bu-gle call like you nev-er heard be-fore, So nat-ur-al that you want to go to war; That's just the best-est band what am,

Valentine's Day

Hearts

and

Flowers

*"My valentine I pray that thou wilt be,
Not for a day, but for eternity."*

—CHARLES NOEL DOUGLAS

Valentine's Day is an ancient holiday with rather uncertain roots. Of the many stories of its origin, two seem the most likely sources for our modern celebration of love. Legend tells of a popular young priest named Valentine who lived in Rome during the reign of Emperor Claudius. The emperor, it is said, was so hungry for war and conquest that he forbade marriages and engagements in Rome to keep the young men free to fight in his armies. Young couples in love turned to Valentine, who, according to legend, performed secret marriages in defiance of the emperor's law. When news of Valentine's weddings reached Claudius, the emperor had him arrested and thrown in jail, where he eventually died on February 14. Another version of the story tells of how the jailed Valentine fell in love with the daughter of his jailer and wrote her a series of letters signed "From your Valentine" before he died.

Whatever the truth of these legends, the name of Valentine became synonymous with messages of love. English poets, playwrights, and essayists—from Chaucer to Shakespeare to Pepys—took up the legend and popularized Valentine as the patron saint of lovers. By the sixteenth century, Valentine's Day was widely observed in Great Britain on February 14. On that day it was customary for lovers to exchange small gifts or notes of affection. In the Victorian era, "valentines," handmade cards decorated with beautiful lace and ribbon carrying messages of love, became the popular gift for the holiday.

Our American Valentine's Day, centering on the exchange of valentines and other tokens of affection, grew out of the English celebration. America's Valentine's Day took off in the early 1800s, when a young female student at Mt. Holyoke College, Esther Howland, began making and selling valentines. Miss Howland, one of the first American businesswomen, imported fine paper and lace and created what became known as "Worcester" valentines, named after the Massachusetts city in which she ran her business. Worcester valentines fed a surge of interest in Valentine's Day, which for a time ranked second only to Christmas as the most popular American holiday. The holiday with such ancient and uncertain origins had found a secure place in American tradition; people of every era, it seems, treasure an occasion to express their most heartfelt emotions.

To My Dear and Loving Husband

ANNE BRADSTREET

If ever two were one, then surely we.
If ever man were lov'd by wife, then thee;
If ever wife were happy in a man,
Compare with me ye women if you can.
I prize thy love more than whole Mines of gold,
Or all the riches that the East doth hold.
My love is such that Rivers cannot quench,
Nor ought but love from thee, give recompense.
Thy love is such I can no way repay,
The heavens reward thee manifold, I pray.
Then while we live, in love lets so persevere,
That when we live no more, we may live ever.

Thine Eyes Still Shined

RALPH WALDO EMERSON

Thine eyes still shined for me, though far
I lonely roved the land or sea:
As I behold yon evening star,
Which yet beholds not me.

This morn I climbed the misty hill
And roamed the pastures through;
How danced thy form before my path
Amidst the deep-eyed dew!

When the redbird spread his sable wing,
And showed his side of flame;
When the rosebud ripened to the rose,
In both I read thy name.

Love, and All That!

JOHN ROLFE BURROUGHS

Her name was Evelyn Ellis, and I first became conscious of her existence while, with several other youngsters, I was skating on Butcherknife Creek where a large concrete conduit carries the stream below the intersection of Sixth and Pine Streets.

We had cleared the snow from the ice both above and below the conduit, but the portion of the creek under cover afforded much the best skating. Even in the daytime it was almost dark in the culvert, which added the spice of adventure to an always exhilarating sport. In the evening, the interior became positively black—so black that, skating through it, you announced your approach with repeated cries of "Look out—here I come!"—your voice assuming the satisfying volume of a lion's roar.

It was here that I discovered that Evelyn Ellis was a *very special person*, that is, someone separate and apart from (and vastly superior to) all other females of the genus *Homo* in the world. She was wearing a red mackinaw-type coat, a red-and-white knit hockey cap, red mittens, and a dark plaid skirt—an altogether entrancing ensemble when portrayed against a backdrop of white snow and blue winter sky. To me, she could skate with far greater ease and grace than any of the other girls.

It was that time of year when the February moon and the evening star are prominent in the heavens even before the sun has gone down; and when the sun does set, the sky immediately fills to overflowing with white and blue and pink stars, all of which twinkle furiously and are diamond bright. In the wintertime in our piece of country, night follows day after only the briefest of interludes.

On this occasion it was getting late, and I should have gone home and done my chores; but, with eyes only for Evelyn Ellis, I kept right on skating. The crowd thinned out until— well, until there were only two people left: Evelyn and I. Skating close, she said "Hello"; and, croaking a couple of times and clearing my throat, I managed a reply. About this time the steam whistle down at the light plant cut loose with the information that it was six o'clock and that I'd best beat it home and milk the cows, but I kept right on skating.

At last Evelyn and I sat down to take off our skates on a bench someone had parked beneath the Butcherknife Tree. We sat there side by side with our shoulders touching for an infinitely precious moment; then she said she guessed she'd better be getting home, and I allowed as how I had too. And so we stood up and started walking, albeit reluctantly.

All of a sudden, Evelyn started to slip on the snowy sidewalk, and I quickly caught her arm. In all the topsy-turviness that followed— skates and scarves flying—she ended up in my arms with her blushing face lifted toward mine. We both awkwardly caught our breath for a second, and then I quickly leaned down and kissed her on the cheek. We scrambled for our skates and started running—Evelyn up Sixth Street, and I down Pine Street.

Even today I can walk down to Sixth Street and, allowing for a three- or four-foot margin of error, locate the memorable spot—this despite the fact that the Butcherknife Tree is no more. But Butcherknife Creek still flows through that same culvert, and the memory of that moment still shines brightly in my mind.

Ask Me Not Why

CORINA R. PIERCEY

Ask me not why I love thee;
No sooner ask the azure sea
Why every day, in white-sailed fleet
Her waves upon the crags do beat.
And if her answer she confide,
Then can I not my secret hide.

Oh, ask not why I love thee,
'Twere wiser, if of yonder tree
You ask the reason for her leaves
When spring is young; why beauty cleaves
To wane in winter. If she tell,
I'll answer why I love thee well.

No, ask not why I love thee,
Wouldst dare to ask the nimble bee
The reason for his hurried flight;
When days are long and summer bright,
Why nature bids him sweetness store?
If he reply, can I say more?

Yet if you would my answer crave,
Then ask not why, but how I love.
And I shall answer, "Not in part;
I love thee, dear, with all my heart."

Not for thy virtues do I care;
Because I love, I find them there.
Nor do I love because of pride;
Pride doth alone in love abide.
But why I love? I cannot tell.
God gave thee me; I know 'tis well.
But be not why, but how, they plea—
With all my heart I cherish thee.

Please Be Mine, Valentine

BEA BOURGEOIS

I've often wondered if my lifelong fascination with mail didn't begin somewhere early in grade school on Valentine's Day. There was always a delicious excitement hidden inside those small white envelopes—even when my name was printed backwards, misspelled, or smudged by the small fingers of my classmates. Would I receive a card from the most popular boy in the room? On the other hand, would the boy I considered a pest send me one? Wouldn't it be wonderful if they both did?

Valentine's Day always generated a lot of fuss when I was a youngster. As first and second graders, we looked forward to the frivolity and bright colors during the dreary, uneventful days of late winter. Beginning early in February, our class discussed the construction of the valentine mailbox, a large cardboard box that we decorated during Friday afternoon art classes.

Covered with red and white crepe paper and festooned with hearts, arrows, and cupids, the finished mailbox occupied a position of honor on a table at the front of the classroom. Red construction paper arrows pointed to the wide slot on top where, on February 14, we would happily deposit our personal stacks of mail.

A week before the day itself, my mother and I would make a special trip to the dime store to buy a box of colorful valentine cards—fifty for nineteen cents. I carefully matched each card to the right classmate before writing his or her name in red across the front of the envelope.

Messages on the "penny" valentines have remained fairly constant through the years: the tall, smiling giraffe proclaiming "Valentine, I long for you"; or a cowboy swinging a lariat and announcing "Valentine, I'd like to steer you my way!"; or a fat, red beet declaring, "Valentine, my heart beets for you!" As a child, I giggled endlessly at every one.

On the fourteenth, smiling children poured into the classroom grasping their newly sealed envelopes. An impressive ceremony always surrounded the delivery of valentines. Several children (usually those with impeccable marks in conduct) were chosen to be the "mailmen" and had the accompanying honor of passing out cards to the rest of the class. The teacher always insisted we go by rows, and each proud mailman would deliver handfuls of valentines to the nervous occupants of rows one through five.

Each year, several mothers "volunteered" (actually, *we* did the volunteering) to provide treats for that afternoon's party. I fondly remember plopping a small candy heart atop each pink cupcake my mother had baked for the festivities. Who would get the heart that said "Wow, Babe" on it? Or the one that said "Hubba Hubba"?

Valentine's Day traditions haven't changed much over the years. The mailbox has been modernized from one large collection depot into individual brown sandwich bags, still decorated with hearts and cupids. Some things don't change, though; the mail is still delivered row by row, and each child still waits nervously for that special card from that certain someone.

I can't remember when we became embarrassed about sending valentines; I suppose it's along about sixth or seventh grade. One's reputation is at stake, after all; and a great deal of teasing might result from sending a particular boy or girl a card that has been designated as "mushy."

Somewhere, though, deep in a dresser drawer, I'm sure there remain many crumpled brown paper bags filled with first-grade wishes and corny rhymes. Perhaps we've saved them to remind us of a corner of childhood that we're all reluctant to part with—a silly and sentimental time when we could ask each and every classmate to "Please Be Mine, Valentine."

To Her

EDGAR A. GUEST

"To the mother of my children
And the faithful wife o' mine,"
That's the line that I shall scribble
On a simple valentine,
Just to sort o' reassure her
In an old man's blundering way
That I'm always thinking of her
Through the troubles of the day.

"To the mother of my children,
And the faithful wife o' mine,"
That's the way that I shall greet her
With some simple valentine.

And her eyes will start to gleamin'
And her heart go pit-a-pat,
For there isn't any title
That would please her more than that.

So it's just that way I'll greet her,
Just to sort o' let her know
That she's still the same old sweetheart
That she was long years ago;
That there's no one any fairer
Than my early valentine,
Now the mother of my children
And the faithful wife o' mine.

Frosted Brownies

Preheat oven to 350° F. Grease and flour a 9-by-12-inch baking pan; set aside. In a double boiler, melt ½ pound sweet butter and 4 ounces unsweetened chocolate over boiling water. When melted, remove from heat and cool to room temperature. In a large bowl, beat 4 eggs and 2 cups granulated sugar until thick. Add 1 teaspoon vanilla. Fold in chocolate mixture and mix thoroughly. Fold in ½ cup sifted, all-purpose flour; mix just until blended. Stir in ⅔ cup walnuts. Pour mixture into prepared pan and bake 25 minutes or until a wooden pick inserted into the center comes out clean; do not overbake. Cool in pan for 30 minutes; cut into bars.

In a double boiler, melt 4 tablespoons sweet butter and 4 ounces semi-sweet chocolate over simmering water, stirring constantly with a wire whisk. Remove pan from heat and beat in 3 tablespoons cream. Sift in ⅔ cup powdered sugar. Add 1 teaspoon vanilla. Stir until very smooth; spread on brownies while frosting is still warm. Makes 28 large brownies.

Always

WORDS AND MUSIC
BY IRVING BERLIN

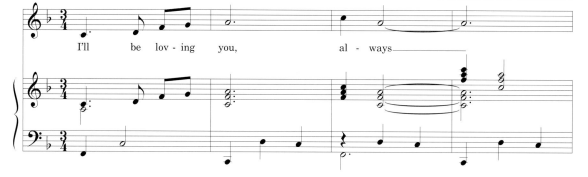

I'll be lov - ing you, al - ways

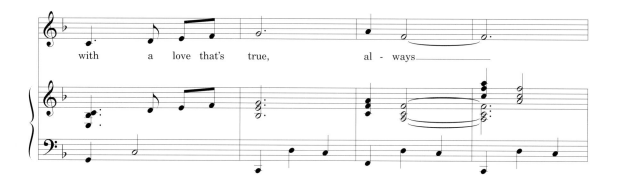

with a love that's true, al - ways

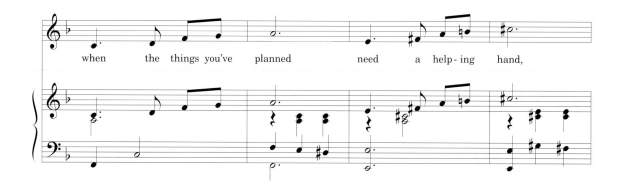

when the things you've planned need a help - ing hand,

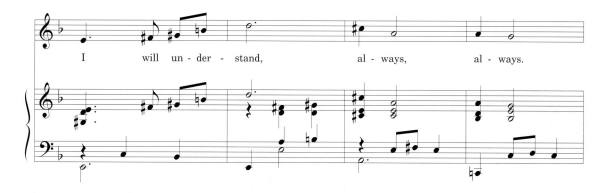

I will un - der - stand, al - ways, al - ways.

Days may not be fair, al - ways.

That's when I'll be there, al - ways,

not for just an hour, not for just a day, not for just a

year, but al - ways. al - ways.

Easter

A

Time of

Renewal

"Faith and Hope triumphant say Christ will rise on Easter Day."

–Phillips Brooks

Easter commemorates the resurrection of Jesus Christ. Through the years, however, customs, symbols, and even words from other times and other countries have enriched our observance to make Easter in America a holy week rich with two thousand years of tradition. Today, Easter continues as the greatest religious day in Christendom; for without it, Christianity itself would have no meaning.

The Gospels tell of Jesus' resurrection; and today's religious observances center around those accounts, such as that in Mark, "And very early in the morning the first day of the week, they came unto the sepulchre at the rising of the sun. . . . and he [an angel] saith unto them, . . . he is risen; he is not here: behold the place where they laid him."

There is no evidence that the first church observed the day of Jesus' resurrection. Within two hundred years, however, some observance of these days began although early Christians disagreed about which day of the week to honor. Christ rose on the "first day of the week" at the time of the Jewish Passover. Christians who had converted from Judaism celebrated Easter on the same date as Passover, regardless of the day of the week. But the Gentile Christians wished to honor the resurrection on Sunday, "the first day of the week." At the Church Council at Nicea, in A.D. 325, the matter was decided in favor of Easter on a Sunday, but still coinciding with the general time of Passover. Today, Christian churches still follow this pattern.

The word *Easter*, however, has nothing to do with the Christian observance. *Eostre*, or *Eastre*, was the name of a pagan goddess of fertility whose ceremony was observed during the same season ancient Romans observed the Feast of the Vernal Equinox, the beginning of spring. Early Christians adopted the name *Easter* and in some respects combined the Roman spring celebration with the religious. Many of these spring symbols remain a part of today's Easter.

For instance, eggs became a popular symbol of Easter. People were forbidden to eat eggs during Lent, so the eggs were saved and served on Easter to break the Lenten fast. Other traditions include Hot Cross Buns served as a Good Friday treat and New York's Easter parade. The parade began at the turn of the century as parishioners emerged from fashionable churches with their new bonnets and turned up Fifth or Park Avenue for a brief walk in the spring sunshine.

Settlers in America celebrated Easter in a number of ways. The Puritans, for instance, were deeply religious but did not observe Easter or Christmas in any manner. The Moravians, who were religious immigrants from Germany, gave to the American culture a unique Easter tradition. In 1741 in Bethlehem, Pennsylvania, the congregation gathered outside the church for the first Easter sunrise service ever. Today, the tradition continues, not only in Moravian churches, but in churches and city parks all over the U.S.

Easter sunrise services are beautiful and inspirational. Poet and songwriter Carrie Jacobs Bond was so moved by an Easter sunrise service that she went home and composed her most well-known song, the beloved "A Perfect Day."

Easter in America is really a week-long observance beginning with Palm Sunday, the Sunday before Easter which commemorates Christ's triumphal entry into Jerusalem. Next comes Good Friday, two days before Easter Sunday, when Christian churches hold solemn services between noon and three o'clock. Finally, Easter Sunday arrives with sunrise services and musical productions, organs and choirs declaring the good news of Christ's victory over death.

He Is Risen!

EDGAR DANIEL KRAMER

"He is risen!" Lo, the grasses
Fill the meadows with their mirth
While the lilacs lift hosannas
As their fragrance fills the earth!

"He is risen!" Lo, the birches
And the oaks high on the hills
Mingle their rejoicing chorus
With the songs of daffodils!

"He is risen!" Lo, the willows,
Leaning where the waters run,
Tremulous, in adulation
Hymn the glory of God's Son!

"He is risen!" Lo, we hearken
To the strangely mystic words
That are filling us with rapture
In the minstrelsy of birds!

"He is risen!" Lo, we echo
Adoration in our eyes
As a host of shining angels
Flings glad songs across the skies!

"He is risen!" Lo, we worship,
Kneeling with each leaf and bloom,
While Lord Jesus leads the springtime
From the darkness of His tomb!

The Open Tomb

In the end of the sabbath, as it began to dawn toward the first day of the week, came Mary Magdalene and the other Mary to see the sepulchre.

And, behold, there was a great earthquake: for the angel of the Lord descended from heaven, and came and rolled back the stone from the door, and sat upon it.

His countenance was like lightning, and his raiment white as snow: And for fear of him the keepers did shake, and became as dead men.

And the angel answered and said unto the women, Fear not ye: for I know that ye seek Jesus, which was crucified.

He is not here: for he is risen, as he said. Come, see the place where the Lord lay. And go quickly, and tell his disciples that he is risen from the dead; and, behold, he goeth before you into Galilee; there shall ye see him: lo, I have told you.

And they departed quickly from the sepulchre with fear and great joy; and did run to bring his disciples word.

And as they went to tell his disciples, behold, Jesus met them, saying, All hail. And they came and held him by the feet, and worshipped him.

Then said Jesus unto them, Be not afraid: go tell my brethren that they go into Galilee, and there shall they see me.

Then the eleven disciples went away into Galilee, into a mountain where Jesus had appointed them.

And when they saw him, they worshipped him: but some doubted.

And Jesus came and spake unto them, saying, All power is given unto me in heaven and in earth.

Go ye therefore, and teach all nations, baptizing them in the name of the Father, and of the Son, and of the Holy Ghost:

Teaching them to observe all things whatsoever I have commanded you: and, lo, I am with you alway, even unto the end of the world. Amen.

Matthew 28:1-10, 16-20

I Shall Remember

ISABELLA WOOD JOHNSTON

I shall remember
   other Easter Days:
The smell of hyacinths,
   a choir song,
The cool, soft drift
   of cherry blooms along
The heartfelt sweetness
   of the April ways,
A sunrise service,
   quietness that prays,
The organ's swell,
   a union in the throng
Of worshippers.
   I shall remember long
The pristine whiteness
   of the lily sprays.

But now that I have walked
   where shadows fall,
I think I'll know this time
   with April's rain
The reason that on Easter Day,
   Christ went
Beside a garden path
   beyond the pall,
And why He walked
   along a country lane.

Easter at the White House

PRISCILLA SAWYER LORD AND DANIEL J. FOLEY

For more than 150 years, since the presidency of James Madison, our nation's Capitol has been the sight of a pleasant Easter pastime—the White House Easter egg roll. Each year, thousands of eager children gather on the pristine White House lawn to roll hard-boiled eggs downhill. The child who retains the last uncracked egg is the winner. The long-lasting tradition is anticipated by many and filled with merriment for all.

The sweeping grounds were thronged, and every moment more were arriving. They came in singles and twos and threes, and they came in a succession of little throngs as streetcar after streetcar unloaded; they came, very many, in motor cars. And in the closed cars the happy little children, gathered half a dozen or so in a car, looked like the crowded nests of brightly plumaged birds, for it was a gathering that included every class. The rich and the well-to-do were there; and the poor were there as well, quite proud of their gayly colored eggs.

There was no formal procedure. Each child carried his or her eggs, all fancifully decorated; and most of them sat quietly on grassy green knolls where their eggs rolled easily.

There was, oddly, a general appearance as if there were only children, for the elders were practically lost, practically unnoticeable, among the gayly colored throng of little ones. Quite amazingly colorful were the children and their accessories: their parasols, their many-colored toy balloons held by strings, the bright baskets, the eggs themselves, the hair ribbons, the jackets and hats and skirts in reds and blues and lavenders, in mustards and pinks. There were children like lilies, all in white, children in pale linen, children like yellow daffodils, seated on the pale green grass.

Some visitors were moving about in gentle happiness. A great fountain was gloriously playing, and all the lilacs were in delicate flower. Intermittently came the music of the Marine Band, and always was the softly chirring sound of children's voices.

The High-Tide of the Year

JAMES RUSSELL LOWELL

Now is the high-tide of the year,
And whatever of life hath ebbed away
Comes flooding back with a ripply cheer
Into every bare inlet and creek and bay.
Now the heart is so full that a drop overfills it;
We are happy now because God wills it.
No matter how barren the past may have been,
'Tis enough for us now that the leaves are green.
We sit in the warm shade and feel right well;
How the sap creeps up and the blossoms swell.

Hot Cross Buns

In a small bowl, soften 1 package dry yeast in ¼ cup warm (120-130° F) water; set aside. In a large bowl, sift together 3½ cups all-purpose flour, 1 teaspoon cinnamon, 1 teaspoon salt, ¼ teaspoon ground cloves, and ¼ teaspoon ground nutmeg. Set aside. In a large saucepan, scald ¾ cup milk; remove from heat and add ½ cup granulated sugar and ¼ cup butter, stir to melt. Cool to lukewarm. Stir in 1 beaten egg and yeast mixture. In a small bowl, sprinkle ¼ cup all-purpose flour over ¾ cup currants. Stir currant mixture into batter along with 2 tablespoons grated lemon peel. Add flour and spice mixture, stirring to make a soft dough. Turn out on a lightly floured board, and let rest 10 minutes. Knead until smooth and elastic, about 5 to 8 minutes. Place in a greased bowl, turning to grease top. Cover and let rise in a warm place until doubled in bulk.

Preheat oven to 375° F. Punch down dough and divide into 3 parts. Divide each third into 6 pieces and roll each into a smooth ball. Place on greased baking sheets with sides of balls touching. Cover and let rise in a warm place until doubled in bulk. In a small bowl, beat 1 egg yolk with 1 tablespoon water. Brush over tops of buns. Bake for 10 to 12 minutes or until golden brown. Remove from baking sheets; cool.

In a small bowl, combine 1 cup powdered sugar, ½ teaspoon vanilla, and 3 to 4 tablespoons water to make a thick frosting. Spread frosting on buns. Makes 18 buns.

Up from the Grave He Arose

WORDS AND MUSIC
BY ROBERT LOWRY

1. Low in the grave He lay, Je-sus my Sav-ior!
2. Vain-ly they watched His bed, Je-sus my Sav-ior!
3. Death can-not keep his prey, Je-sus my Sav-ior!

Wait-ing the com-ing day, Je-sus my Lord!
Vain-ly they sealed the dead, Je-sus my Lord!
He tore the bars a-way, Je-sus my Lord!

Up from the grave He a-rose, He a-rose, With a might-y tri-umph o'er His foes; He a-rose, He a-rose!

rose a vic-tor from the dark do-main, And He lives for-ev-er with His saints to reign. He a-

rose! He a-rose! Hal-le-lu-jah! Christ a-rose! He a-rose! He a-rose!

Mother's Day

MEMORIES

OF

MOTHER

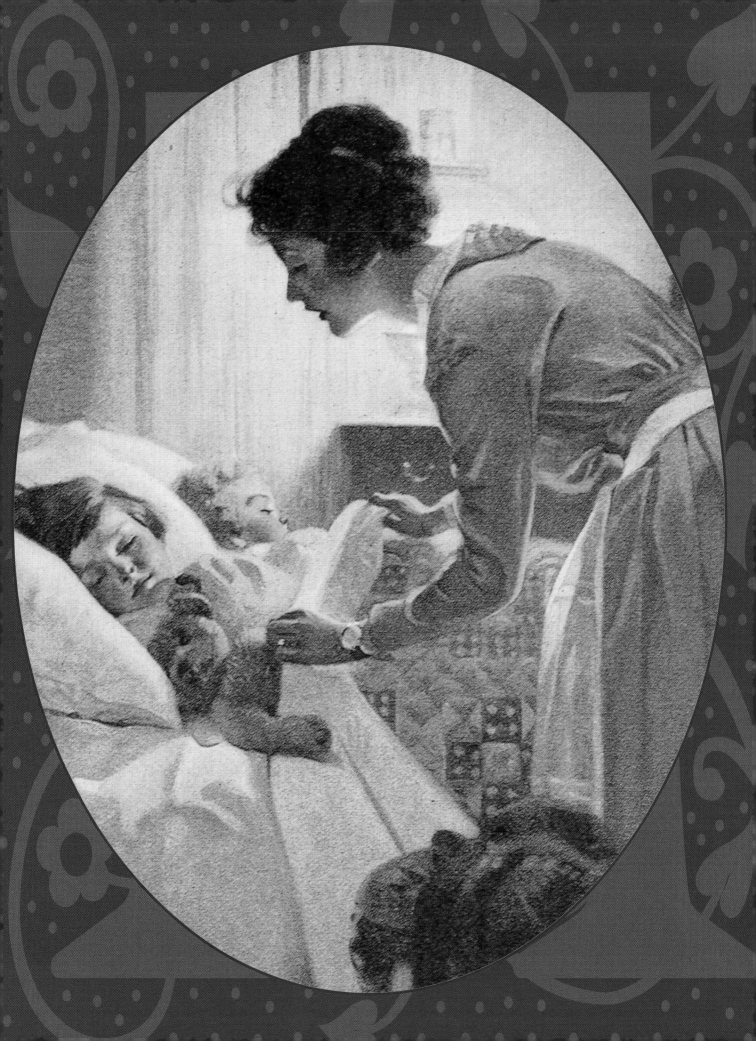

> *"All that I am or hope to be,*
> *I owe to my angel mother."*
>
> –ABRAHAM LINCOLN

Long before the birth of our great nation, England celebrated a special day for mothers on what was called "Mothering Sunday." The traditions for that day included a visit to Mother to deliver a fresh-baked cake made especially for her.

Years later, in 1907, a young woman named Anne Jarvis felt compelled to begin a similar tradition in the United States. Miss Jarvis began a nationwide letter-writing campaign of heartfelt pleas to members of Congress and Americans of all walks of life to set aside a special day honoring mothers. A devoted daughter, Miss Jarvis had lost her own dear mother a few years earlier, and she hoped to persuade others to recognize the importance of all mothers' love and dedication. On May 10, 1908, the third anniversary of her mother's death, Miss Jarvis asked her church to hold a special service in honor of mothers everywhere. The church members enthusiastically agreed; and each of those in attendance was given a white carnation, the favorite flower of Miss Jarvis's beloved mother.

Due in great part to Miss Jarvis's efforts, the idea of celebrating Mother's Day spread rapidly throughout the country. At first, the day was observed most often in special church programs.

Then various governors began issuing Mother's Day proclamations and encouraging people to visit or write their mothers on this holiday, and soon all states in the nation were observing Mother's Day. The tradition of wearing a carnation spread as well—red carnations were worn by those whose mothers were living; and white carnations, symbolizing sweetness, purity, and endurance, were worn by those whose mothers had died.

By 1914, celebrating Mother's Day had become so popular that Congress, in recognition of the influence mothers have in the making of better citizens, recommended that the second Sunday in May be called Mother's Day from that date forward. President Woodrow Wilson then issued a proclamation, asking that the American people display the flag on that day "as a public expression of our love and reverence for the mothers of our country." From coast to coast, Americans hoisted their flags and sent their mothers messages of love to celebrate the day. Anne Jarvis saw her devotion to her own mother grow into a nationwide celebration filled with traditional gifts, joyous visits, and special memories—all in honor of the deserving individuals we call mothers.

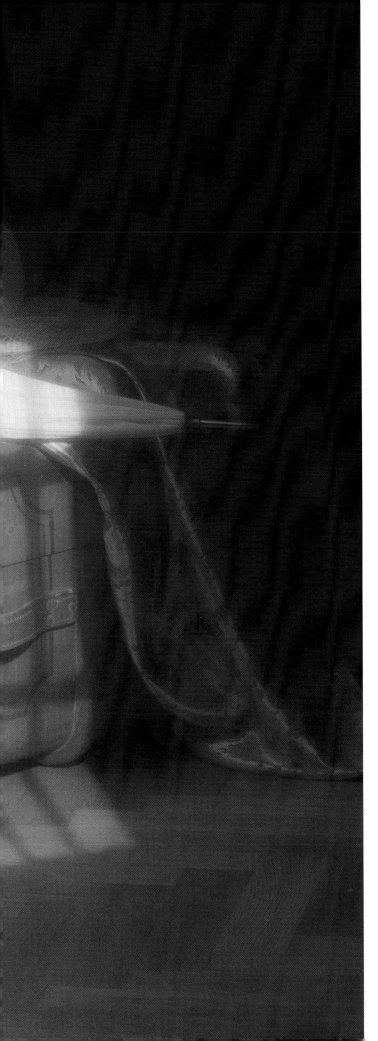

A Mother-Song

JAMES WHITCOMB RILEY

Mother, O Mother! Forever I cry for you,
Sing the old song I may never forget;
Even in slumber I murmur and sigh for you.
Mother, O Mother,
Sing low, "Little brother,
Sleep, for thy mother bends over thee yet!"

Mother, O Mother! The years are so lonely,
Filled but with weariness, doubt and regret!
Can't you come back to me, for tonight only,
Mother, my mother,
And sing, "Little brother,
Sleep, for thy mother bends over thee yet!"

Mother, O Mother! Of old I had never
One wish denied me, nor trouble to fret;
Now must I cry out all vainly forever,
Mother, sweet Mother,
O sing, "Little brother,
Sleep, for thy mother bends over thee yet!"

Mother, O Mother! Must longing and sorrow
Leave me in darkness, with eyes ever wet,
And never the hope of a meeting tomorrow?
Answer me, Mother,
And sing, "Little brother,
Sleep, for thy mother bends over thee yet!"

Mother's Day

MARJORIE HOLMES

"S ometimes I wish they'd dispense with Mother's Day," the woman said to the teen-ager. "I know my children love me; I wish they didn't feel they have to go out and spend their money on cards and gifts.

"Then, too, as an adult I love my own mother dearly and enjoy doing things for her, but Mother's Day makes it an obligation. Not because she expects anything or would be hurt if it weren't forthcoming, but because the advertisers have made it almost a must."

The girl looked back with a kind of troubled astonishment. "Why, I suppose," she said. "I just never thought of it like that. I mean, from a young person's point of view, it's fun. I like buying my mother a gift—especially now that I'm earning my own money. This year I'm getting her a lovely nightgown and a corsage. I've been thinking about it all week and looking forward to getting paid so that I could."

Suddenly the event falls into new perspective. Why, of course. Mother's Day, like practically every other holiday, is for the children!

The dancing eyes, the secrets. The giggling, "Stay out of my room!" The pot holders woven at school and hidden under a bed, the kindergarten's crepe paper carnations.

And a small girl's sly, "Have you got some material I could use? I mean *big* material, big enough for a big person to wear if somebody was going to make that person a dress?" And submitting to being measured around the waist and draped in an ancient rose print you've dug out of the attic. And warning, "Dear, it's pretty hard to make a dress. I mean you ought to be older and have a pattern."

And the blithe reply born out of the miracle of faith and love, "Oh, I don't need any pattern. I can see it in my mind just as plain—how pretty you'll look in this dress." Aghast at this revelation, she claps her hand over her mouth while you pretend not to have heard.

And a son's dragging you to the drugstore to "look around" while he slips proudly up to the cosmetic counter to spend a whole dollar on cologne.

No, there's no out for us. Even the people who originally thought up Mother's Day probably got a greater glow out of it than their mothers. Gazing at the heap of presents, nibbling burned toast eagerly served in bed, many a mother will secretly agree, "It is more blessed to give than to receive."

But her heart will be full, nonetheless. For she in her own way knows the pleasure of giving pleasure—by simply being the object and center of all this.

This is her special secret on Mother's Day. This is the part she plays in the sweet conspiracy of love.

Happy Mother's Day

A Mother's Love

GRACE NOLL CROWELL

I have not found the word,
 I cannot find
One single phrase
 to satisfy my mind
Or any synonym
 that might express
A mother's love—
 that love with the power to bless
The life of any child
 within her care,
An expended love,
 and yet enough to share
With other children
 if there be a need.
Elastic, tender is that love,
 indeed.

It is spent, yet saved;
 it is emptied, yet filled up
As steady rain will brim
 an upheld cup.
It is gentle
 and yet tiger-fierce when harm
Threatens her young
 through any quick alarm.
It is selfless as the love
 of Christ for men.
It is holy, it is beautiful,
 but when
The seeking heart strives
 to define its worth,
There is no word for it
 in heaven or earth!

The Legacy

ALICE MASON

She could not give her children gold,
So she gave them faith to have and hold.
She could not give them royal birth,
A name renowned throughout the earth;
But she gave them seeds and a garden spot
And shade trees when the sun was hot.
She could not give a silver spoon
Or servants waiting night and noon.
She gave them love and a listening ear

And told them God was always near.
She could not give them ocean trips
Aboard majestic sailing ships,
But she gave them books and a quiet time,
Adventures found in prose and rhyme.
She could not give them worldly things,
But what she gave was fit for kings.
For with her faith and books and sod
She made each child aware of God.

My Mother's Hands

CARRIE M. ADAMSON

I can't remember when first I saw my mother's hands. Perhaps it was my first day of school. I clung to her hand that day as she walked with me down the sidewalk, and I was most reluctant to part with the security her hand represented.

Or was it, I wonder, one of the fall afternoons when I rushed home from school to find her in the warm, sweet-smelling kitchen, where she was taking her homemade bread from the oven? (No gourmet dinner could ever compare with those thick slices of hot buttered bread that she doled out graciously to my brothers and me!)

It could have been the winter when I was ten years old and her cool, competent hands gently nursed me through a serious bout with scarlet fever. Then, again, perhaps it was the day her deft fingers gave me a final fitting in the formal she had patiently made for the senior prom, or the morning of my wedding day when I found her tenderly pressing my bridal veil.

I don't remember when I first *really* saw my mother's hands, but certainly it must have been when she was bestowing largess! They're gentle hands, and tender, unadorned except for the thin, gold wedding band she has worn for almost half a century. They're small, but can move mountains; they're graceful, but not strangers to hard work. In age, they're resigned. In prayer, they're at peace. In need, they're resourceful. In sickness, they're comfort.

No, I don't remember when I first saw my mother's hands, but I need only close my eyes to see them now; and they're a symbol of all that's reassuring and right in the world.

Nobody Knows But Mother

MARY MORRISON

How many buttons are missing today?
    Nobody knows but Mother.
How many playthings are strewn in her way?
Nobody knows but Mother.
How many thimbles and spools has she missed?
How many burns on each fat little fist?
How many bumps to be cuddled and kissed?
    Nobody knows but Mother.

How many hats has she hunted today?
    Nobody knows but Mother.
Carelessly hiding themselves in the hay,
Nobody knows but Mother.
How many handkerchiefs willfully strayed?
How many ribbons for each little maid?
How for her care can a mother be paid?
    Nobody knows but Mother.

How many muddy shoes all in a row?
    Nobody knows but Mother.
How many stockings to darn, do you know?
Nobody knows but Mother.

How many little torn aprons to mend?
How many hours of toil must she spend?
What is the time when her day's work shall end?
    Nobody knows but Mother.

How many lunches for Tommy and Sam?
    Nobody knows but Mother.
Cookies and apples and blackberry jam—
Nobody knows but Mother.
Nourishing dainties for every "sweet tooth,"
Toddling Dottie or dignified Ruth—
How much love sweetens the labor, forsooth?
    Nobody knows but Mother.

How many cares does a mother's heart know?
    Nobody knows but Mother.
How many joys from her mother-love flow?
Nobody knows but Mother.
How many prayers for each little white bed?
How many tears for her babes has she shed?
How many kisses for each curly head?
    Nobody knows but Mother.

Mom's Lemon Drizzle Cake

Preheat oven to 350° F. In a medium bowl, sift together 3 cups all-purpose flour, 2 teaspoons baking powder, and ¼ teaspoon salt; set aside. In a large bowl, cream 1 cup softened butter with 2 cups granulated sugar until light and fluffy. Add 4 eggs; beat well. Stir in flour mixture alternately with 1 cup sour cream; blend well. Stir in 1 tablespoon grated lemon peel and 1½ cups raisins. Pour batter into a greased and floured, 10-inch tube pan. Bake 1 hour and 15 minutes or until wooden pick inserted into center comes out clean. Cool 10 minutes in pan on wire rack. Place on cake plate.

In a small bowl, combine ⅓ cup lemon juice and ¾ cup granulated sugar; blend well. Brush mixture on hot cake; let cool. Makes 12 servings.

M-o-t-h-e-r

HOWARD JOHNSON

THEODORE MORSE

"M" is for the mil - lion things she gave me, "O" means on - ly that she's grow - ing
"M" is for the mer - cy she pos - ses - es, "O" means that I owe her all I

old, "T" is for the tears were shed to save me,
own, "T" is for her ten - der sweet car - res - ses,

"H" is for her heart of pur - est gold. "E" is for her eyes, with love-light
"H" is for her hands that made a home. "E" means ev -'ry-thing she's done to

shin - ing, "R" means right, and right she'll al - ways be.
help me, "R" means real and reg - u - lar, you see.

Put them all to-geth-er, they spell Moth - er! A word that means the world to me.

Decoration Day

Remembering

Those Who Came

Before Us

"To live in hearts we leave behind is not to die."

–THOMAS CAMPBELL

The American celebration of Decoration Day (or Memorial Day) dates back to the days immediately following the end of the Civil War, when a compassionate gesture by a group of Mississippi women resonated throughout the nation and gave birth to a movement toward a national day for honoring the memory of those who gave their lives in battle. America was deeply wounded and sharply divided in late April of 1865. The Civil War had ended weeks before; but in cities and towns across the nation families mourned their fallen, and the resentment between Union and Confederate, between North and South, still ran deep. When a group of women in Columbus, Mississippi, announced their intention to march together to Friendship Cemetery on the outskirts of town and lay flowers on the graves of the men—Union and Confederate alike—who had died at the Battle of Shiloh, town elders resisted. They were not prepared to put the passions of the war behind them. But the women were adamant; they marched to the cemetery on April 26, 1865, and decorated the graves of all the fallen soldiers with beautiful spring blossoms.

News of Mississippi's Decoration Day, as it became known, spread quickly. In New York City, a young man named Francis Miles Finch read a notice of the event in the New York *Tribune*. Mr. Finch, moved by the Mississippi women's spirit of compassion and forgiveness, wrote a poem commemorating the occasion.

"The Blue and the Gray" immortalized the laying of flowers "alike for the friend and the foe"; its haunting lines helped the nation heal and helped Americans understand the need for a national day of remembrance.

Memorial Day as we know it today grew slowly from the original Decoration Day. In 1868, the Grand Army of the Republic, an organization of Union veterans, declared May 30 a day for "strewing with flowers or otherwise decorating the graves of comrades who died." In 1873, New York became the first state to recognize Memorial Day as an official holiday for honoring Civil War dead; others soon followed. With the passage of time, as more wars and more battles claimed the lives of brave Americans, Memorial Day became a holiday for honoring all those who gave their lives in service; and eventually, for remembering all lost loved ones.

Today, on the last Monday in May, cemeteries fill with families bearing beautiful spring blossoms for the graves of those they have lost. Like the women of Mississippi, who rose above prejudice and resentment with a gesture of true respect for the sanctity of all life, a gesture which in honoring the past created hope for the future, those who decorate the graves of the departed on Decoration Day with spring flowers—symbols of life renewed—honor the lives of those who came before them and acknowledge their own responsibility to those who will come after.

Memorial Day

EDGAR A. GUEST

Blow gently, winds of May,
And softly stir the trees,
Whispering today
The love we bear to these
Who sleep that silent sleep,
At rest forevermore.
Blow gently, winds of May;
Their warfare is now o'er.

Blow gently, winds of May,
Bearing perfume rare
Of blossoms o'er the way;
Rose petals scatter there;
The starry flag we place
In glory on each grave,
Catches in a fond embrace
For us and proudly waves.

Blow gently, winds of May;
Shine softly summer sun.
Our heroes sleep today,
Their duty nobly done.
And with the flag they loved
And flowers, we come today
To honor those who sleep.
Blow gently, winds of May.

Lilacs for Memorial Day

ROSE KORALEWSKY

The lush grass deepens by forgotten roads
Where little vagrant breezes softly stray,
Laden with fragrance from the leafy bowers
Where blossom lilacs for Memorial Day.

The dewy sprays of Tyrian rose and white
Still nod above the stone walls old and gray,
As once when happy children laughed with joy
To see the lilacs for Memorial Day.

Gone are the ancient houses mossy-roofed,
Gone the white schoolhouse where in brave array
The bright-eyed boys and girls once proudly marched,
Bearing their lilacs for Memorial Day.

The spirit still lives on that burned in those
For whom at flowery shrines we kneel and pray,
Though now neath low green tents they dreamless sleep,
Covered with lilacs for Memorial Day.

The volleys and the bugle notes are stilled,
And bright flags flutter in the sun's last ray.
Once more they bloom on fair New England hills—
The hallowed lilacs for Memorial Day.

The Trumpet Contest

DR. DONALD R. STOLTZ

It was a beautiful spring day in Elmville, and there was a feeling of excitement and electricity in the air. Robert Prince was up early. He jumped out of bed to look from his window at the clear, blue sky and the morning sun sparkling through the tiny, green leaves that were just beginning to appear on the trees.

Today was the day that Robert had waited for. Ever since that morning about two months before when he had seen the sign on the bulletin board at school, he had been able to think of nothing else. He could still picture it in his mind: "Notice: Memorial Day Parade. Trumpet players needed for town band. Tryouts May 15, 1921."

For two years Robert had been taking trumpet lessons. Although his music teacher told him he was playing very well, he knew that the chance to play in the town band was a big step. What a thrill to be all dressed up in a bright red uniform with a high hat and big, brass buttons, marching right down Main Street. It would be a glorious feeling to march through the park to the bandstand by the lake for the Decoration Day concert.

Robert grabbed his trumpet, which he had carefully polished for two hours the day before, and started toward the big gazebo in the center of Elmville Park, where he learned that thirteen musicians were trying out for only two positions. Rob was a bit nervous, but confident all the same. When his name was called, he took out his music sheet, took a deep breath, and began to blow. The sound was sharp and clear and loud; his performance was flawless.

When he was finished, he glanced over at the panel of judges; and his eyes suddenly became fixed upon a familiar face. It couldn't be, but it was! It was Mr. Sailor, his music teacher, who had not told Robert that he was to be a judge. Wow! How could he lose now? Robert sat down with a relaxed and secure feeling of victory.

Finally the competition ended, and it was time to announce the winners. Robert listened intently for his name to be called; but moments later, two other names were announced. Robert sat back in a state of shock. "I just can't believe it," he thought. "The way I played! The errors that the others made! And my teacher was one of the judges! How could I lose? With his head bent down on his hands, he thought how badly this important day had turned out.

Suddenly a familiar voice spoke up behind him. "That was a splendid performance, lad. The best by far," Mr. Sailor bellowed. "I'm proud of you, Rob. You must have had a great teacher!" he added with a thunderous laugh.

"Mr. Sailor," Rob said softly, "If you and I are so good, how did I lose?"

"You didn't lose, my boy. You just won the most important contest of your life. Just as we were about to choose the winners for the contest, an old friend of mine came over to the judges' stand. I used to play the trumpet in his band many years ago. It was the best band then, and it is the best band now. He wanted to know who you were and if you were free for the summer. Are you?"

"Well, yes. I guess, of course, yes, I am," Robert stuttered. His heart was pounding.

"Good, then you have yourself a job, boy. You see, you didn't lose a contest; you've won yourself a full-fledged position in the finest band in the land. You'll be playing in parades in different towns and in concerts in beautiful parks every summer. I couldn't let you win that contest and have you waste your time and talent playing that bugle in Elmville all summer, so I chose someone else as the winner. Oh, here comes my friend now! John, this is Robert Prince, your new trumpet player; and Robert, I want you to meet your new boss, Mr. John Philip Sousa."

Best Home-Fried Chicken

Rinse one 3- to 3½-pound, cut-up, skinless frying chicken. Soak pieces in saltwater 30 minutes. Dry thoroughly with paper towels. In a medium bowl, place 1 cup unbleached, all-purpose flour. Add 1 teaspoon dried thyme and ½ teaspoon black pepper. Coat chicken by rolling pieces in the seasoned flour or by tossing them with the flour in a plastic bag. Before frying, shake the pieces to remove any excess flour. In a heavy frying pan, add enough vegetable shortening to come to a depth of about ½ inch. When the fat is hot, but not smoking, add the chicken, largest pieces first. Do not crowd. Fry over medium-high heat, turning pieces to brown all sides. When all sides are golden, reduce heat to low, add ½ cup water, and cover pan. Cook gently 45 minutes. Remove cover, increase heat to medium. As the flour coating turns crispy, gently turn pieces, making sure that the flour coating does not stick to pan. Serve hot. Store in refrigerator. Makes 4 to 6 servings.

Potato Salad

Scrub 10 tiny new potatoes well with a soft brush. Cut into chunks and drop into a kettle of cold, salted water. Bring to a boil and cook until tender but still firm, 8 to 10 minutes. Meanwhile, chop ¼ pound bacon and sauté until crisp. Remove bacon and set aside. In remaining bacon fat, sauté ¼ cup finely chopped shallots until tender but not browned, approximately 5 minutes. Reserve shallots and fat. When the potatoes are done, drain and drop into a mixing bowl. In a small bowl, combine ¼ cup red wine vinegar, 2 tablespoons olive oil, shallots, and reserved bacon fat. Pour over the hot potatoes. Season with salt and pepper to taste. Gently toss to mix. Stir in ¼ cup chopped red onion, 1 teaspoon ground celery seed, and ½ cup chopped fresh parsley and toss again. Sprinkle reserved bacon on top. Serve at room temperature. Store refrigerated. Makes 4 servings.

AMERICA **77** CELEBRATES

The Battle Hymn of the Republic

JULIA WARD HOWE   MUSIC TRADITIONAL

Mine eyes have seen the glo - ry of the com - ing of the Lord; He is tram - pling out the vin - tage where the grapes of wrath are stored; He hath loosed the fate - ful light - ning of His ter - ri - ble swift sword: His truth is march - ing on.

CHORUS

Glo - ry! Glo - ry! Hal - le - lu - jah! Glo - ry! Glo - ry! Glo - ry! Hal - le - lu - jah! Glo - ry! Glo - ry! Hal - le - lu - jah! His truth is march - ing on.

Father's Day

In

Praise of

Father

"A father is a guiding light sent to us from above."

–Byron P. Tousignant

The celebration of Father's Day grew out of the devotion of two individuals who, half a continent apart, expressed their deep appreciation for their own fathers by working to establish a special day of recognition for all fathers. Sonora Smart Dodd of Spokane, Washington, and Harry Meek of Chicago never met, nor is there any indication that either one knew of the other; yet their parallel efforts brought the need for a special day for fathers to the nation's attention.

Sonora Smart Dodd first envisioned a national Father's Day while sitting in church on Mother's Day in 1910. Mrs. Dodd had lost her mother at an early age; and she, along with five younger brothers, had been raised by her devoted and loving father, William Jackson Smart. As her minister praised the community's mothers, Mrs. Dodd thought naturally of her own father and the sacrifices he made to raise his children. Later that year, Mrs. Dodd wrote to the local YMCA and the Spokane Ministerial Association and suggested that Spokane honor fathers with a special day. The community took to her idea immediately and settled upon the third Sunday in June 1911 as their first Father's Day. The day was marked in community churches by special sermons on the role of fathers and by the wearing of roses—red for a living father, white for one deceased.

Mrs. Dodd's Father's Day quickly became an established tradition in Spokane and much of Washington, but the holiday was still unknown in Chicago in 1915 when Harry Meek, president of the Uptown Lions Club, suggested a day to honor fathers in his community. The idea took hold; and Chicago, by pure coincidence, also began celebrating Father's Day on the third Sunday in June. For two decades, Harry Meek wrote letters to the president lobbying for an official national holiday. In 1924, President Calvin Coolidge responded with full support, but no official proclamation. Coolidge recommended that all Americans observe Father's Day "to establish more intimate relations between fathers and their children and also to impress upon fathers the full measure of their responsibility."

From two independent starts, in Washington and in Chicago, Father's Day grew into a nationwide celebration. By April 24, 1972, when President Richard Nixon signed a joint Congressional resolution setting aside the third Sunday in June as a day of recognition and honor for American fathers, the shared dream of Mrs. Dodd and Mr. Meek had already been fulfilled; Father's Day was firmly established in American tradition and fondly embraced by all Americans who had known the love and care of a devoted father.

Patterned Ways

ROY Z. KEMP

I shall walk in my father's steps,
Not because it is easy,
But because I like the deep marks
He always makes. They are easy to follow,
Whether I trudge behind him in the snow,
Through tall grasses, along the dunes,
Or follow him through his plowed furrows.

When I was small, I had to stretch
My legs to match his stride.
Sometimes I failed,
But always I tried.

He shows no sign,
Nor has he ever shown a sign,
He is aware of this, my following.
He sets his patterned mark for me;
And filled with pride, I bravely follow him.

Now having grown a bit,
I tread behind
With ease. Occasionally,
Unless I watch myself,
I walk with even longer stride
And overreach his tracks,
Making new ones of my own.

God grant that I shall mark
A patterned way
As clear for my own son.

Dear Dad

CHARLES S. KINNISON

However rich the soil may be
In which a tree may root,
It cannot reach maturity
And bear its finest fruit
On what it draws from earth below.
It also needs the sky,
A guiding light, a friendly glow;
And like that tree am I.

A Father's Job

EDGAR A. GUEST

I may not be as clever as my neighbor down the street;
I may never be as wealthy as some other men I meet;
I may never have the glory that some other men have had;
But I've got to be successful as this little fellow's dad.

There are certain dreams I cherish that I'd like to see come true;
There are things I would accomplish ere my working time is through;
But the task my heart is set on is to guide a little lad
And to make myself successful as this little fellow's dad.

I may never come to glory; I may never gather gold;
Men may count me as a failure when my business life is told.
But if he who follows after shall be manly, I'll be glad;
For I'll know I've been successful as this little fellow's dad.

It's the one job that I dream of; it's the task I think of most.
If I'd fail that growing youngster, I'd have nothing else to boast;
For though wealth and fame I'd gather, all my future would be sad
If I failed to be successful as this little fellow's dad.

The Father

VIOLET ALLEYN STOREY

I thank you, God, for life's command to work.
That I, each day, must touch the wheel of things.
I thank you for the coming of the night,
The firelight and the dream-edged thoughts it brings.
My gratitude for seasons in their turn,
For holidays when I may stay at home,
For speech and laughter and the love of friends,
For pungent promises of new turned loam.
But most of all I thank you that a child
Can see in me the man he hopes to be
And that a woman with an angel's heart
Has deigned to share a mortal's lot with me.

Peach Cobbler

Preheat oven to 400° F. Peel and slice 4 cups ripe, fresh peaches; arrange in a greased, 2-quart baking dish. Sprinkle with ⅔ cup granulated sugar, 1 teaspoon grated lemon peel, 1 tablespoon fresh lemon juice, and ¼ teaspoon almond extract. Bake 20 minutes. In a large bowl, sift together 1½ cups unbleached, all-purpose flour; 1 tablespoon granulated sugar; 1 tablespoon baking powder; and ½ teaspoon salt. Cut in ¾ cup shortening until mixture resembles cornmeal. In a small bowl, combine 1 egg, lightly beaten, with ¼ cup milk; stir into dry ingredients just until moistened. Remove peaches from oven and quickly drop dough by large spoonfuls over the surface. Sprinkle with 2 tablespoons granulated sugar. Return to oven 15 to 20 minutes or until top is firm and golden brown.

In a large bowl, whip 1 cup heavy cream to soft peaks. Stir in 1 tablespoon powdered sugar and ½ teaspoon vanilla. Serve cobbler warm with whipped cream. Makes 6 servings.

The Crunch of Gravel

PHILIP B. KUNHARDT, JR.

At times I think back to my childhood again, to our lives on the hill which were made up of a network of little routines and rituals. Weekdays passed slowly; we counted them on our fingers, all of us gathering in a bunch each morning to wave good-bye to my father as he chugged Celeste (one of his many cars through the years) out of the garage, made her roar and smoke, then shot down the drive to disappear in the green trees, his hand hurling kisses behind. When we were on vacation from school, my brother and I would be out at the garage before him, tugging up the old door on its ungreased tracks, there for a hug when he came charging out of the house. We would run beside the car for a final slap at the rumble seat or the back fender to see who could have the last tap.

In the summer, he would be back home when it was still light, to work in his gardens till the petals on his roses lost their color; but in early spring and in late fall and all winter long, he came home in the dark. We waited for his headlights and the crunch of gravel his tires made before we streamed out to the garage again to hurl ourselves upon him. He took his time getting to the house, checking on his flower beds which ran along the carpenter's shop. If it were winter, he would stop to shake off the stooping load from his box bushes, check on his bird feed tray, look out over his garden to the twinkling valley way beyond, and breath slow, deep breaths; for he was happy to be at his home again.

His evening rituals were slow, deliberate. Off with hat about halfway between garage and house, loosen tie if it were summer, up the three porch steps, open screen door, let it bang behind, now the heel of a hand to the dark green wood of the front door which always stuck, the clack of the knocker as it got shaken by the opening of the door, the stamping off of snow on the porch. Open wide now and in and hello to everyone.

People coming from all over the house to say hello, my mother from the top of the stairs, calling and rushing down, and all of us children, if we had not been outside, streaking down the banister backwards and being plucked off at the end and hugged.

Off with the rubbers now, or the arctics, standing over by the tiny hall radiator, a lot of hopping on one foot to get the blasted things off, a pat for Hundy, who knew a friend when he saw one and waggled a brown ear against my father's trouser leg. Soon his hat joined all the other lids of the house on top of the hall chest.

Now open the gorilla closet underneath the stairs. Force coat onto the packed bar, head disappearing for a moment among all those camphor coats, a sudden pounding against the back of the closet, a growl, jumping back, slamming the door shut and leaning on it. "He almost got me then, that old Egor," my father would say, panting fright. We never saw the wild, ferocious gorilla, Egor, that lived back in there somewhere in the closet; but he was surely there—didn't he growl and pound every evening when my father disturbed him again?

The evening ritual continued. Up the stairs, squeeze left through the tiny hall. Unload pockets onto the top of the highboy. Gold pocket watch and chain with gold penknife at the other end. Pennies, nickels, dimes and quarters. Subway tokens. Wallet. Letters of the day. I had to get a chair to see it all—spread out there with the cuff links and the tie clips, the half-gone roll of peppermint candies, the gold pen and pencil, the little black leather date book, the horn-rimmed reading glasses, the bits of paper and notes and dollar bills and odds and ends and all the other secrets of his business day.

That was about it on weekdays—nothing really special at all, yet quite a bit special, and quite a lot to be remembered.

A Different Style of Saint

J. R. PICI

I remember my father best, T-shirted and hair askew, out in the backyard where crushed grass formed a diamond. He pitched a white whiffle ball and sometimes gave me four strikes and batted left-handed against me and never threw too hard or ran too fast. When I hit a screamer off the roof (it was a homer from the bedroom window to the chimney), he'd shout with glee then kick the imaginary mound, muttering he'd get me next time, as I proudly circled the bases, swearing I could hear a thousand cheers.

We played endless innings until fireflies speckled the outfield. Then, after three "one-more-swings," he'd gather the bat and ball in one hand and me in the other and carry us back to the house. At night, my only light the iridescent dial of a radio carrying games from far-off roaring stadiums, I'd dream of going four for five against the fabulous Phillies in the World Series of the universe.

But that time passed, as time has a habit of doing. Then there were Huck Finn and Tom Sawyer. And then there were Moby Dick and Hemingway. Then there were somber term papers and moralistic letters to the editor. And somewhere along the way, crossing bridges I hadn't dreamed of, I garnered that same enthusiasm of my lost youth for the world of real fiction.

I am now a teacher, of which my mother is quite proud. As for my father, he scoffs at my bookish devotion. But often I find him hunched over a dog-eared book he has taken from my room, and a sweet chill runs up my spine. He's a different style of saint, I think. Then just the other day, after a silent supper, an orange rolled off the table. My father scooped it cleanly on the short hop and placed it back in the fruit bowl. We looked at each other shyly, smiling and remembering days of innocent illusions, of driving home in the dark after bat days at the park, of falling asleep with my head in his lap. Of days crowded only with us, gone too soon, passed too fast.

Daddy's Little Girl

WORDS AND MUSIC
BY BOBBY BURKE AND HORACE GERLACH

You're the end of the rain-bow, my pot o' gold, You're Dad-dy's Lit-tle Girl to have and hold. A pre-cious gem is what you are, you're Mom-my's bright and shin-ing star.

You're the
You're the

Independence Day

Parades

and

Picnics

"Day of
Flags
and Cannon
and Jubilee"!
uarded well,
gloried in,
o may it ever be.

JULY 4th

Fire Works

KEEP DRY

Ellen H. Clapsaddle

"For what avail the plow or sail,
Or land or life, if freedom fail?"

–RALPH WALDO EMERSON

In a letter to his wife, Abigail Adams, written in July of 1776, Continental Congress member John Adams predicted that future generations would celebrate July 2 with "solemn acts of devotion to God Almighty . . . with pomp and parade, with shows, games, sports, guns, bells, bonfires, and illuminations, from one end of this country to the other." On July 2, 1776, the Second Continental Congress, meeting at Philadelphia, had adopted, by a 12-0 vote with New York abstaining, the resolution by Richard Henry Lee of Virginia that "these united colonies are, and of right ought to be, free and independent states." The colonies had declared independence, and John Adams recognized it as a momentous event in history.

Americans proved Adams's prediction of an annual July celebration of Independence Day correct, although they chose July the fourth, not the second, as their day of revelry and tribute. It was on July 4, 1776, that Richard Henry Lee's resolution found stirring, eloquent, and public expression in Thomas Jefferson's Declaration of Independence. Jefferson had begun work on the Declaration in early June; John Adams and Benjamin Franklin then suggested improvements on his first draft and, in the early days of July,

the entire Congress gave the document some fine tuning. On July 4, 1776, the Congress gave final approval to the document that proclaimed to the world the colonies' reasons for declaring independence.

The glorious news of the Declaration's adoption spread rapidly from Philadelphia to all the eager colonists—all, that is, except for those in Williamsburg, the colonial capital of Virginia, who did not receive the news until July 25, 1776. To this day, the people of Williamsburg celebrate Independence Day three weeks later than the rest of the nation.

The thirteen colonies had been at war with Great Britain since April of 1775, but it was not until the Declaration of Independence that the war became openly and officially about separation and independence. On July 4, 1776, the Declaration of Independence gave voice to the revolutionary belief that citizens had inalienable rights and that rulers derived their power from the consent of those they governed. Americans rightly chose this day as their day of independence; and for more than two hundred years, they have honored the tradition with joyous "pomp and parade" as John Adams had so perfectly predicted.

Old Ironsides

OLIVER WENDELL HOLMES

Ay, tear her tattered ensign down!
Long has it waved on high,
And many an eye has danced to see
That banner in the sky;
Beneath it rung the battle-shout,
And burst the cannon's roar:
The meteor of the ocean air
Shall sweep the clouds no more!

Her deck, once red with heroes' blood,
Where knelt the vanquished foe,
When winds were hurrying o'er the flood
And waves were white below,
No more shall feel the victor's tread,
Or know the conquered knee:
The harpies of the shore shall pluck
The eagle of the sea!

Oh, better that her shattered hulk
Should sink beneath the wave!
Her thunders shook the mighty deep,
And there should be her grave.
Nail to the mast her holy flag,
Set every threadbare sail,
And give her to the god of storms,
The lightning and the gale!

One of Boston's very special Independence Day traditions and one of the most popular musical events in the country is the Boston Pops Annual Fourth of July concert. This two-hour concert's finale, a rousing rendition of the 1812 Overture, is replete with thunderous cannons. To close the day, a dazzling display of fireworks lights the sky over the Charles River, near where the USS Constitution ("Old Ironsides") rests today.

Independence Day

PAMELA KENNEDY

Independence Day is about a lot more than freedom from Mother England. For me, it has as much to do with my freedom to be young again, to do silly things, and to enjoy simple pleasures that America has to offer. It has to do with remembering a time when I couldn't see moon dust up close or fly faster than the speed of sound. In short, I can be a kid again on the Fourth of July! At first I thought this was a personal discovery, but over the years I have learned that it is not. People all over the country love to drop the mantle of sophistication and get down to serious silliness on the Fourth.

One hot July Fourth in a suburb north of Chicago, I sat on a curb to watch the "World Famous (so they said) Precision Mower Drill team." Twenty men, dressed in trench coats and fedoras, marched in columns, each pushing a power lawn mower. It was a deafening chorus of Black and Deckers and Craftsmen executing fancy maneuvers up Main Street. Bankers, lawyers, and doctors, mind you, mowing asphalt in eighty-degree weather, grinning like kids out of school—only on the Fourth of July.

In Milwaukee on another Independence Day, we witnessed "The Largest (they claimed) Kazoo Marching Band in the Entire U.S. of A." One hundred folks marched past in Groucho glasses, complete with oversize nose and mustache, belting out a nasal version of "Stars and Stripes Forever." On any other day of the year, you couldn't persuade even one of them to walk a block playing the kazoo. But on the Fourth of July, the ridiculous becomes sublime.

This thought returned to me at our most recent neighborhood Fourth of July extravaganza. Early in the day we gathered at the community pool to witness feats of skill and agility. The favorite event consisted of two teams battling valiantly to win in a contest based loosely on water polo. The big difference was, of course, the ball—in this case a ten pound watermelon coated with shortening. There were cheers and jeers as the "Vegematics" team finally squirted the melon to victory!

We hardly had time to catch our breath before the fire truck arrived to take interested parties for a ride. No matter if we were over forty, we eagerly climbed up and made the siren go! Some of us had waited decades for the thrill of this moment. On the Fourth of July, the child in each of us would not be denied!

There were over-done burgers and charcoal-striped hot dogs for supper with corn on the cob, and thick, drippy slices of watermelon. Naval officers who at other times dined with admirals and ambassadors licked their sticky fingers and then lined up for an impromptu seed spitting contest. The victor got to pick first when we chose sides for the annual tug-of-war.

As the sun began to set, the tugging teams positioned themselves. Tension mounted, the rope stretched taut over a great puddle of mud; at the signal, the pulling began. Traditionalists favored the organized chant and pull technique, while the avant-garde contingent screamed like banshees and dashed back and forth, throwing off the timing of the opposition. I don't remember who won, but there were plenty of muddy bodies when the competition ended, along with plenty of accusations about cheating and squashed toes. Shortly, things degenerated into a good-natured, mud-slinging free-for-all.

As darkness fell, we gathered—muddy, tired, and stuffed—to watch the fireworks. Children's wonder filled us again as the multi-colored star showers exploded in the sky. I held hands with my middle-aged, mud-caked husband. Tomorrow, we would be businesslike and grown up again: neat, tidy, and responsible. But tonight, under the star-spangled sky, we were kids once more. Tonight was the Fourth of July!

America for Me

HENRY VAN DYKE

'Tis fine to see the Old World
And travel up and down
Among the famous palaces
And cities of renown,
To admire the crumbly castles
And statues of the kings;
But now I think I've had enough
Of antiquated things.

So it's home again, and home again,
America for me!
My heart is turning home again,
And there I long to be,
In the land of youth and freedom
Beyond the ocean bars
Where the air is full of sunlight
And the flag is full of stars.

I know that Europe's wonderful,
Yet something seems to lack!
The past is too much with her,
And the people looking back.
But the glory of the present
Is to make the future free—
We love our land for what she is
And what she is to be.

Oh, it's home again, and home again,
America for me!
I want a ship that's westward bound
To plow the rolling sea,
To the blessed land of room enough
Beyond the ocean bars,
Where the air is full of sunlight
And the flag is full of stars.

Homemade Vanilla Ice Cream

In a large, heavy saucepan, combine 1⅓ cups milk and 2⅔ cups heavy cream. Add ½ vanilla bean, split. Bring almost to a boil. Reduce heat and simmer 5 minutes. Slightly beat 8 egg yolks; whisk yolks together with 1 cup granulated sugar until mixture is smooth and sugar is dissolved. Remove milk mixture from heat; remove vanilla bean and whisk 1 cup hot milk gradually but thoroughly into egg yolks. Stir well, then whisk egg mixture into milk. Return saucepan to stove and cook over low heat, whisking constantly, just until custard thickens; do not let it boil. Strain custard. Cool and chill well. Transfer to ice cream maker and freeze according to manufacturer's instructions. Makes 1½ quarts.

Classic Carrot Cake with Cream Cheese Frosting

Preheat oven to 350° F. Grease two 9-inch layer cake pans and line with wax paper; set aside. Sift together 3 cups all-purpose flour, 3 cups granulated sugar, 1 teaspoon salt, 1 tablespoon baking soda, and 1 tablespoon cinnamon. Add 1½ cups vegetable oil, 4 lightly beaten eggs, and 1 tablespoon vanilla. Beat well. Fold in 1½ cups chopped walnuts; 1½ cups shredded coconut; 1⅓ cups puréed, cooked carrots; and ¾ cup drained, crushed pineapple. Pour batter into prepared pans. Bake on middle oven rack 20 to 35 minutes or until edges have pulled away from sides and a wooden pick inserted into center comes out clean. Turn out on wire rack; cool 3 hours. Meanwhile, cream one 8-ounce package cream cheese at room temperature with 6 tablespoons butter. Slowly sift in 3 cups powdered sugar and continue beating until smooth. Stir in 1 teaspoon vanilla and juice of ½ lemon. Fill middle and frost sides and top. Makes 10 to 12 servings.

Independence Bell

AUTHOR UNKNOWN

There was a tumult in the city
In the quaint old Quaker town,
And the streets were rife with people
Pacing restless up and down—
People gathering at corners,
Where they whispered each to each,
And the sweat stood on their temples
With the earnestness of speech.

So they surged against the State House,
While all solemnly inside,
Sat the Continental Congress,
Truth and reason for their guide,
O'er a simple scroll debating,
Which, though simple it might be,
Yet should shake the cliffs of England
With the thunders of the free.

Hushed the people's swelling murmur,
Whilst the boy cries joyously;
"Ring!" he shouts, "Ring! Grandpapa,
Ring! Oh, ring for Liberty!"
Quickly, at the given signal
The old bellman lifts his hand,
Forth he sends the good news, making
Iron music through the land.

That old State House bell is silent,
Hushed is now its clamorous tongue;
But the spirit it awakened
Still is living—ever young;
And when we greet the smiling sunlight
On the fourth of each July,
We will ne'er forget the bellman
Who, betwixt the earth and sky,
Rung out, loudly, "Independence";
Which, please God, shall never die!

You're a Grand Old Flag

**WORDS AND MUSIC
BY GEORGE M. COHAN**

You're a grand old flag, you're a high fly-ing flag, and for-ev-er in peace may you

wave; You're the em-blem of the land I love, the

home of the free and the brave. Ev-'ry heart beats true un-der

Red, White and Blue, where there's nev-er a boast or brag: "But should

auld ac-quain-tance be for-got," keep your eye on the grand old flag.

Labor Day

The Last

Lazy Day

of Summer

"The labourer is worthy of his reward"

–I Timothy 5:18

In 1882, Peter J. McGuire, founder and president of the United Brotherhood of Carpenters and Joiners of America, calling American workers the "great vital force of the nation," proposed that the first Monday in September be celebrated as Labor Day, a "general holiday for the working classes." In a speech to the New York Central Labor Union, McGuire suggested a "festive day during which a parade through the streets of the city would permit public tribute to American industry."

McGuire, the tenth child of Irish-American parents, began working in piano and furniture factories when he was just eleven years old. He understood the life of the laborer from the inside out and was one of many labor leaders who were fighting to improve conditions for America's workers. Since the beginning of the industrial revolution, workers had suffered through six- or seven-day work weeks and twelve hour days, through poor and often dangerous conditions, all with no job security, no benefits, and low pay. After the Civil War, labor unions began to form in America. They gave a powerful voice to the common workers and forced significant reforms in factories. McGuire's idea for a national Labor Day captured the spirit of the newly empowered American worker.

Peter McGuire was an eloquent, passionate, and convincing speaker; his idea for a Labor Day was immediately embraced by the workers of New York City. On September 5, 1882, more than ten thousand workers left their jobs and joined in a parade through the streets of New York, followed by an afternoon of picnics and speeches and evening fireworks. A new American tradition was begun. By 1894, Labor Day was a legal holiday in thirty states. In that year, recognizing America's desire to salute its workers, President Grover Cleveland signed the holiday into national law. Today, Labor Day is an anticipated time when American workers in all fields can relax with friends and family, bid farewell to summer, and enjoy a well-deserved day of rest.

September

GLADYS TABER

Now in September the rhythm of life changes; for summer's lease, as Shakespeare said, hath all too short a date. The air is soft, seductive; twilights are dreamy; at night, stars candle the sky. Gardens still bloom; there will be some roses until the black frost. The Cape goldenrod spreads rusty gold along winding roadsides. Hal Borland once counted the blossoms on the sweet goldenrod that grows inland and came up with 3,023 in one spray. Here the flower heads are even denser and darker, sturdy against the sea winds.

But two main changes take place. Gardeners rush to pick the late corn, bring in summer squash, harvest the crisp string beans, and fill the salad bowl with the last lettuce and green

pepper. They discover that fried tomatoes in cream gravy have not lost their charm. A few dig potatoes the size of marbles and make a whole meal of new potatoes doused in milk, butter, seasoned salt, and pepper. The state of the beach plums is the main topic of conversation.

The second change is the end-of-summer migration across the bridge. Cars are crammed with children, dogs, luggage, sleeping bags, boxes of shells still smelling of the sea, and sometimes bicycles, canoes, and fishing gear precariously lashed on the cartop or hanging behind in a trailer. School is just ahead, so fathers and mothers haul reluctant sun-browned children from the beach, catch the family pet

(who vanished when he heard the word *suit-case*), and turn in the keys for the rented cottage.

"Do we really have to go back so soon? Why can't we stay a little longer?"

"You have to go to the dentist before school opens, remember. And you have to have new shoes." Besides, Daddy has to get back to work. In many cases, Mommy does too. At the very least, she has plenty of household chores to attend to before everybody is settled in for autumn.

It is a melancholy procession, bumper to bumper all the way to the canal, where the bridge writes the final signature of Cape Cod against the pale September sky.

Plea to September

SYLVIA TRENT AUXIER

Prelude of Autumn, on your two-toned trees
Foretell her glory to the south, and spill
The goldenrod's bright promises in seas
Of molten color down each rolling hill.
Smile into bloom the nodding crimson clovers
And ardent roses only June should own;
And let the summer's flitting, faithless lovers
Kiss to brief being moments that have flown.

But, O September, leave securely curled
In every branch's brown and curving scroll
The vanished Spring's green secrets; and leave furled
The lilac's plume of fragrance. Do not call
The heart to hold within its small recess
Both Autumn's glory and Spring's loveliness.

Mysterious Patterns

MAY SMITH WHITE

The day grew quiet here, no ripples played
Upon the austere sky. And golden leaves
Hung motionless, as if each one obeyed
The pattern set when browning Autumn grieves.
But soon each leaf will yield itself to earth,
Weaving a russet carpet once again;
And autumn fires will then come into birth,
Quenched later by the cold November rain.

Here lie the mysteries that Autumn keeps.
And through this time, her songs will lull the heart
While plans grow richer as all nature sleeps,
Because her deftness is her counterpart.
With changing seasons, I still yearn to see
The sign of Autumn in the maple tree!

Who Love the Autumn

Dana Kneeland Akers

They who love the autumn
Scuff with wayward feet
Where the yellowed windrows
By ash and elm are laid,
Savoring the incense
From fires along the street,
Pausing in the darkness
To watch the embers fade.

Windows dressed in scarlet, russet,
Gold, and brown;
Bough and sheaf and pumpkin,
Set for Halloween.
Bring the season's color
To invest the town,
Poor in Autumn's substance
With something of her sheen.

Place has no distinction,
Leaves against the curb,
Rain on bleaching stubble,
Avenues grown bare—
All possess enchantment to charm
And yet disturb.
They who love the autumn
Find it everywhere!

"School" from Lake Wobegon Days

GARRISON KEILLOR

School started the day after Labor Day, Tuesday—the Tuesday when my grandfather went, and in 1918 my father, and in 1948 me. It was the same day, in the same brick schoolhouse, the former New Albion Academy, now named Nelson School. The same misty painting of George Washington looked down on us all from above the blackboard, next to his closest friend, Abraham Lincoln. Lincoln was kind and patient, and we looked to him for sympathy. Washington looked as if he had a headache. His mouth was set in a prim, pained expression of disapproval. Maybe people made fun of him for his long, frizzy hair, which resembled our teacher's, Mrs. Meiers's, and that had soured his disposition. She said he had bad teeth—a good lesson to remember: to brush after every meal, up and down, thirty times.

The great men held the room in their gaze, even the back corner by the windows. I bent over my desk, trying to make fat vowels sit on the line like fruit, the tails of consonants hang below, and colored the maps of English and French empires, and memorized arithmetic tables and state capitals and major exports of many lands and when I was stumped, looked up to see George Washington's sour look and Lincoln's of pity and friendship, an old married couple on the wall. School, their old home, smelled of powerful floor wax and disinfectant, the smell of patriotism.

Mine was a vintage desk with iron scrollwork on the sides, an empty inkwell on top, a shelf below, lumps of petrified gum on the underside of it, and some ancient inscriptions, one from '94 ("Lew P.") that made me think how old I'd be in '94 (fifty-two) and wonder who would have my place. I thought of leaving that child a message. A slip of paper stuck in a crack: "Hello. September 9, 1952. I'm in the fifth grade. It's sunny today. We had wieners for lunch and we played pom-pom-pullaway at recess. We are studying England. I hope you are well and enjoy school. If you find this, let me know. I'm fifty-two years old."

It took me a long time to learn to read. I was wrong about so many words. *Cat, can't. Tough, through, thought. Shinola.* It was like reading a cloud of mosquitoes. Donna in the seat behind whispered right answers to me, and I learned to be a good guesser; but I didn't read well until Mrs. Meiers took me in hand.

One winter day she took me aside and said she'd like me to stay after school and read to her. "You have such a nice voice," she said, "and I don't get to hear you read as much as I'd like." No one had told me before that I had a nice voice. She told me many times over the next few months what a *wonderful* voice I had as I sat in a chair by her desk reading to her as she marked papers. "The little duck was so happy. He ran to the barn and shouted, 'Come! Look! The ice is gone from the pond!' Finally it was spring."

"Oh, you read that so well. Read it again," she said. When Bill the janitor came in to mop, she said, "Listen to this. Doesn't this boy have a good voice?" He sat down, and I read to them both. "The little duck climbed to the top of the big rock and looked down at the clear blue water. 'Now I am going to fly,' he said to himself. And he jumped and—" I read in my clear blue voice. "I think you're right," Bill said. "I think he has a very good voice. I wouldn't mind sitting here all day and listening to him."

Labor Day

Edgar A. Guest

They're the source of all our greatness
    who are keeping Labor Day.
From their skill and strength and knowledge
    came the splendors we display.
For that "know how" which we boast of
    when there's something to be done
Is the wisdom of the millions
    who together work as one.

It's our nation that is pausing
    for a little while today
To picnic with the children
    and to romp the time away.
On this dedicated Monday
    unto labor, I can see
In the parks and on the benches
    freedom's surest guarantee.

It's our country that is resting,
    and the workers keep it great.
They're the strength of every city;
    they're the might of every state.
They're the source of every triumph;
    they're the strong and skillful host
That will conquer every challenge
    to the things we cherish most.

Holiday

MARY MCDONALD

Dress the kids and keep them clean.
Keep them where they can be seen.
Make the salad, bake the cake,
Gather everything to take.
Fry the chicken, pack the box,
Bring along some extra socks.
Grab the coats and mop the floor.
Last one's out, so lock the door.
Each one's finally in the car.
Lucky that the park's not far.
Now I know, to my dismay,
Why they call it Labor Day.

Best-Ever Bread Pudding

Crumble 1 loaf stale French bread into a large bowl. Pour 4 cups milk over bread and set aside 1 hour. Preheat oven to 325° F. In a medium bowl, beat 3 eggs, 1 to 1½ cups granulated sugar, and 2 tablespoons vanilla. Stir into bread mixture. Add 1 cup raisins, mixing well. Pour into a buttered 9-by-13-by-2-inch baking dish. Bake on middle oven rack until browned and set, about 70 minutes. Cool to room temperature. In top of double boiler, stir 8 tablespoons butter and 1 cup powdered sugar until sugar is dissolved and mixture is hot. Remove from heat. Whisk 1 beaten egg into sugar mixture. Remove pan from water base; continue beating until sauce has cooled to room temperature. Stir in 3 teaspoons orange extract. Serve warm. Makes 8 to 10 servings.

September Song

MAXWELL ANDERSON　　　　　　　　　　　　　　　　　**KURT WEILL**

Oh it's a long, long while From May to De - cem - ber.

But the days grow short when you reach Sep - tem - ber.

When the au - tumn wea - ther turns the leaves to flame,

One has - n't got time for the wait - ing game.

Oh, the days dwin-dle down _____ to a pre - cious few,

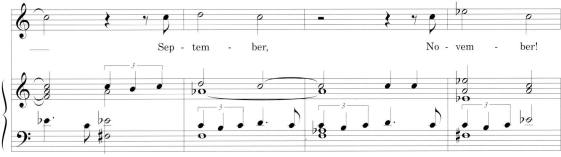

____ Sep - tem - ber, No - vem - ber!

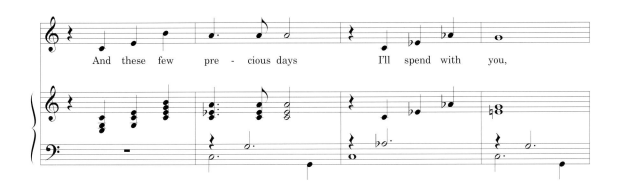

And these few pre - cious days I'll spend with you,

These pre-cious days I'll spend with you. _____

Thanksgiving

A Family

Gathering at

Harvesttime

"Thanks unto the harvests' Lord who sends our daily bread."

–ALICE WILLIAMS BROTHERTON

In November of 1621, the residents of Plimoth Plantation, a Massachusetts Bay settlement of English religious separatists known as Pilgrims, celebrated a feast of thanksgiving. In the year since their arrival in the New World, the brave Pilgrims had seen forty-three of their 103 perish. They had endured a winter colder and harsher than anything they had ever imagined. They had cleared the heavily forested land by hand and built small homes. They had made peace with the local native people and, with their help, planted corn and barley. They had watched and worked and prayed all summer as their food supply dwindled and their new crops grew. By November, with a bountiful harvest in and a secure village built, the Pilgrims were ready to pause and give thanks with a great feast. It is this feast that Americans fondly cherish as the very first Thanksgiving Day.

It was, however, more than 150 years before the modern tradition of a Thanksgiving Day each November took root. The Pilgrims celebrated subsequent feasts of thanksgiving; and as settlements developed into colonies and spread inland and down the coast, such days of thanks were common, but irregular. Giving thanks became an established tradition, but the holiday as we know it remained nonexistent.

Thanksgiving's history as an official holiday began in 1789 when President George Washington called for a national Thanksgiving Day in honor of the newly signed Constitution, which guaranteed civil and religious freedom in the new nation. "It is the duty of nations to acknowledge," the president wrote, "the providence of Almighty God, to obey His will, to be grateful for His benefits, and humbly to implore His protection." In the following years, Thanksgiving was celebrated sporadically and regionally; it did not become an annual tradition until the Civil War, when the threat to the Union's survival made Americans more aware than ever of the blessings of their citizenship.

Sarah Josepha Hale, editor of the popular *Godey's Lady's Book*, had been promoting a national Thanksgiving Day since 1846. With the Civil War on, she urged Americans to begin such a day as "a renewed pledge of love and loyalty to the Constitution of the United States." In 1863, President Abraham Lincoln, buoyed by the Union victory at Gettysburg and hopeful for the survival of the Union, proclaimed a national Thanksgiving Day on the last Thursday in November. The president urged Americans to give thanks for God's guidance and for the survival of their Union. From that year forward, presidents regularly issued Thanksgiving Day proclamations. By the 1930s, the holiday was so firmly entrenched in American tradition that President Franklin Roosevelt's attempt to move it back a week, to provide more time between Thanksgiving and Christmas, met with a public outcry. The holiday was returned to the last Thursday in November, where it remains today.

An annual, modern-day harvest feast at Plimoth Plantation, a living museum in Plymouth, Massachusetts, re-creates the meal in 1621 that became the model for our own Thanksgiving Day celebrations. The re-creation reflects all the known details of the original feast, including the colonists' dialect and clothing as well as the recipes and table setting for the bountiful meal. This harvest feast reminds Americans of the trials and joys of our Pilgrim ancestors and the reasons for their thankful hearts that long-ago autumn. It offers a connection through time as Americans of yesterday and today give thanks for our many blessings.

The Landing of the Pilgrims

Felicia D. Hemans

The breaking waves dashed high
On a stern and rock-bound coast;
And the woods against a stormy sky
Their giant branches tossed;

And the heavy night hung dark
The hills and water o'er
When a band of exiles moored their bark
On the wild New England shore.

Not as the conqueror comes,
They, the true-hearted, came;
Not with the roll of the stirring drums
And the trumpet that sings of fame;

Not as the flying come,
In silence and in fear;
They shook the depths of the desert gloom
With their hymns of lofty cheer.

Amidst the storm they sang,
And the stars heard, and the sea;
And the sounding aisles of the dim woods rang
To the anthem of the free.

The ocean eagle soared
From his nest by the white eave's foam.
And the rocking pines of the forest roared;
This was their welcome home.

Ay, call it holy ground,
The soil where first they trod;
They have left unstained what there they found,
Freedom to worship God.

The Sumac Leaves

JONES VERY

Some autumn leaves a painter took
And with his colors caught their hues;
So true to nature did they look
That none to praise them could refuse.

The yellow mingling with the red
Shone beauteous in their bright decay;
And round a golden radiance shed,
Like that which hangs o'er parting day.

Their sister leaves, that, fair as these,
Thus far had shared a common lot,
All soiled and scattered by the breeze
Are now by everyone forgot.

Soon, trodden under foot of men,
Their very forms will cease to be,
Nor they remembered be again
Till Autumn decks once more the tree.

But these shall still their beauty boast,
To praise the painter's wondrous art,
When Autumn's glories all are lost
And with the fading year depart.

And through the wintry months so pale
The sumac's brilliant hues recall;
Where, waving over hill and vale,
They gave its splendor to our fall.

Thanksgiving

GLADYS TABER

Thinking back to when my own daughter was an earnest little Pilgrim in the school pageant, I can still hear that piping voice practicing her recitation over and over:

"In sixteen hundred and twenty
On a rough and barren coast
The Pil'rims started a 'settle-mint'
And established a trading post."

And I can still remember the despair that swept through the entire family on the morning of the great performance when we discovered that there wasn't a single large-sized safety pin anywhere in the house and that the waistband of my crepe skirt, the most essential item in her costume, couldn't be fastened snugly in any other way. I can't remember how we solved the problem. I suspect that her teacher, being an old hand at school productions, had an emergency kit full of safety pins and sewing supplies.

When my granddaughters reached that age, Alice, too, was a Pilgrim in white paper collar and cuffs, while Anne was lucky enough to be a Wampanoag squaw and got to paint her face with red and yellow streaks.

However, except in the schools, the story of the first Thanksgiving seems to be taken pretty much for granted. Of course, the churches will be bright with autumn foliage and glowing displays of seasonal fruits and vegetables, and the service will center on our gratitude for all that God has given us during the past year and our need to share our bounty with those who are less fortunate. And when the whole family gathers around the dinner table, we will feel, as always, a special thankfulness that we can all be together once again.

But what will we talk about? An unusual recipe for pumpkin pie, a football game, a piece of family news, the latest headlines? How many of us will even think of the old story that explains how this celebration of Thanksgiving first began?

I have just been reading a book based on William Bradford's own account, and I am surprised to find out how little I know about the original holiday. The Pilgrims were not celebrating a very good harvest, it turns out. Their twenty acres of corn had done well (thanks to Squanto), but their six or seven acres of English crops—peas, barley, and wheat—had failed. Bradford comments cautiously that this was due either to "ye badness of ye seed, or latenes of ye season, or both, or some other defecte." All the same, they were able to increase the weekly food ration a little: in addition to one peck of meal per person (from the *Mayflower*'s supplies), they now received one peck of maize. Eleven buildings had been finished, relations with the Indians were peaceful, and there had been no illness for some months. All this was reason enough to declare a holiday so that, as Bradford puts it, they might "after a more special manner, rejoyce together."

So they set the date—it was in October—and sent an invitation to Massasoit. They were somewhat dismayed when he turned up with ninety braves, but the great chief dispatched several hunters into the forest and before long was able to contribute five deer to the feast. (It is a welcome guest who brings a gift of food!) In addition, the menu included roast goose, roast duck, eels, clams, and other shellfish, two kinds of bread—white and corn—and bowls of crisp watercress, leeks, and other "sallet greens." There is no record that the Pilgrims ate any of the wild turkeys they saw running in the woods

or the cranberries that filled nearby bogs. Neither is there any mention of pumpkin pie; for dessert they had wild plums and dried berries.

All in all, it was a fine holiday. The feasting went on for three days, Captain Miles Standish staged a parade, both Pilgrims and Indians played games of skill and chance, and there was probably plenty of singing and dancing. The celebration was such a success, in fact, that it was repeated every year. But it was not until 1863, in the middle of the Civil War, that Abraham Lincoln proclaimed it a national holiday and set aside the date in November.

The first Thanksgiving was hardly over, however, when the Pilgrims discovered that they had grossly overestimated their harvest. The meager weekly ration had to be cut in half, and people braced themselves for another grueling winter. Still, they did not lose hope; with God's help, they would survive.

The lesson is worth remembering, I think. Especially when life seems grim, it is good to be reminded of those early New Englanders: of their courage and fortitude—and their faith.

And so the cherished holiday is here again, with the traditional turkey and giblet gravy, snowy mashed potatoes, tender-sweet turnips, golden squash, and pumpkin pie. In the country, children roast chestnuts over the hearth fire. In the city, street vendors pop the shiny brown nuts over braziers. When day is done, parents and grandparents reminisce, happy over shared memories. Children have a way of idling into the kitchen because cold turkey has a special charm. And the puppy and kitten are already at the refrigerator door.

"Turkey is my favorite food of all," one of the grandchildren says dreamily. "That and lobster."

And it occurs to me that courage takes many forms. Crossing the seas calls for one sort—it is heroic and we remember it. But who was the man who first dared toss a lobster on a bed of coals and discover the delicate pink-white richness inside?

Thanksgiving Time

STELLA CRAFT TREMBLE

The Autumn season finishes the year,
Hangs harvest moon in cooler atmosphere.
Grain ripens, wheat and oats leap into shocks,
We hasten toward the year's last equinox.

For Winter hides behind a northern sky,
Floats in each wavering wind that flurries by.
Thanksgiving time, corn hurries toward the barn
As ice forms isles on meadow-brook and tarn.

At borderland of every fertile field,
Marauding crows peck at remaining yield
Of grain dropped by machine or man, unseen.
They chatter as they sweep the furrows clean.

Apples, like small, red worlds, plunge down the night
On orchards, in mounds beautiful and bright;
Fall changes little as the years go by.
The prairie folk are glad, and so am I.

For every single blessing gives a reason
That we rejoice at this Thanksgiving season!

Sweet Potato Casserole with Walnuts

Preheat oven to 350° F. In a large bowl, place 4 cups cooked and mashed sweet potatoes; one 8-ounce package cream cheese, softened; ½ cup unsalted butter, softened; 2 eggs, beaten; ¼ cup brown sugar; 2 tablespoons orange juice; 1 tablespoon grated orange peel; ¼ teaspoon ground cinnamon; and ¼ teaspoon salt. With an electric mixer, whip all ingredients until light. Stir in ¾ cup chopped black walnuts. Spoon mixture into a buttered casserole dish. Spread evenly and sprinkle with ½ teaspoon grated nutmeg. Bake 45 minutes or until golden. Makes 8 servings.

Patty's Cranberry Fluff

Grind 1 pound fresh cranberries and place in a large bowl. Add 1 cup granulated sugar and mix well. Refrigerate 2 hours. In a large bowl, beat 1 pint heavy cream until stiff. Fold in 3 cups miniature marshmallows. Fold cranberry mixture into whipped cream. Stir in one 1-pound can drained, crushed pineapple and ½ cup chopped pecans. Makes 8 to 10 servings.

Baked Indian Pudding

Preheat oven to 350° F. In a large bowl, combine 1 cup yellow granulated corn meal, ½ cup black molasses, ¼ cup granulated sugar, ¼ cup butter, ¼ teaspoon salt, ¼ teaspoon baking soda, 2 eggs, and 3 cups hot milk. Pour mixture into an oven-proof, 3-quart casserole dish. Bake until mixture boils. Remove and stir in an additional 3 cups hot milk. Return to the oven; lower temperature to 250° F. Bake 4 to 4½ hours. When it is done, the pudding should be smooth, not gritty. Makes 6 to 8 servings.

For All the Blessings of the Year

ALBERT H. HUTCHINSON   **ROBERT N. QUAILE**

Christmas

ALL HEARTS

GO HOME

AT CHRISTMAS

"All of us hear the angels for a little while at Christmas."

–ELISABETH BORROWES

And they came with haste, and found Mary, and Joseph, and the babe, lying in a manger." Thus the shepherds began the celebration of Christmas. Americans celebrate the birthday of Jesus Christ with traditions brought to us from various countries and with some uniquely American customs as well.

In the southern colonies, the planters brought to the New World the customs of their homeland, mainly England. The season was filled with gay balls and bountiful feasts. The Yule log burned, mistletoe and greenery hung in the doorways and over the mantles, and caroling was heard throughout the land. In the Northeast, however, the Puritan settlers forbade any observance of Christ's birth and levied fines on those who dared celebrate the holiday. It was not until the nineteenth century, after the arrival of many German and Irish immigrants, that holiday celebrations became popular in the northern part of the country.

One group coming to our shores from Germany was the Moravians, some of whom settled in Old Salem, North Carolina. They still observe the holiday with the Moravian Lovefeast, an eighteenth-century revival of the early Christian *agape*—the breaking of bread together by believers to signify their union and equality (not to be confused with the Lord's Supper). The Lovefeast is a special time of music, the Christmas story, and lighted candles.

Moravian Christmas Eve services, like other Christian services, feature candlelighting ceremonies. In a darkened church, each person is given a lighted candle tied with a red band. The light represents the flame of love, whereas the red band represents the blood of Christ shed for their redemption. Today, Moravian Christmas Eve services in Old Salem constitute a lovely part of our heritage.

Singing carols is a favorite part of the holiday celebration, and Americans have added magnificent carols to the world's hymnals. Minister Phillips Brooks wrote "O Little Town of Bethlehem," and poet Henry Wadsworth Longfellow penned "I Heard the Bells on Christmas Day." Spirituals from African-Americans also add to our rich music heritage with "Rise Up, Shepherd, and Follow" and "Jehovah, Hallelujah, the Lord Will Provide."

Some of the more charming secular Christmas traditions deal with Santa Claus, whose name came from the German mispronunciation of St. Nicholas. Thomas Nast, a German immigrant and cartoonist, first depicted Santa Claus with a sleigh and reindeer. But when Dr. Clement C. Moore wrote a delightful poem for his son, who was sick in bed on Christmas Eve, the image of Santa Claus was immortalized. Entitled "The Night Before Christmas," this poem described Santa to the world and created a legend.

Nowhere in the world is Christmas as diverse as in America. The traditions brought by settlers and immigrants more than two hundred years ago have made our heritage richer by the blending. Traditions continue to form in the hope that "peace on earth, goodwill to all men" will become a reality, at least at Christmastime in America.

The Nativity

And it came to pass in those days, that there went out a decree from Caesar Augustus, that all the world should be taxed. And all went to be taxed, every one into his own city. And Joseph also went up from Galilee, out of the city of Nazareth, into Judaea, unto the city of David, which is called Bethlehem; (because he was of the house and lineage of David:) to be taxed with Mary his espoused wife, being great with child.

And so it was, that, while they were there, the days were accomplished that she should be delivered. And she brought forth her firstborn son, and wrapped him in swaddling clothes, and laid him in a manger; because there was no room for them in the inn.

And there were in the same country shepherds abiding in the field, keeping watch over their flock by night. And, lo, the angel of the Lord came upon them, and the glory of the Lord shone round about them: and they were sore afraid. And the angel said unto them, Fear not: for, behold, I bring you good tidings of great joy, which shall be to all people. For unto you is born this day in the city of David a Saviour, which is Christ the Lord.

And this shall be a sign unto you; Ye shall find the babe wrapped in swaddling clothes, lying in a manger. And suddenly there was with the angel a multitude of the heavenly host praising God, and saying, Glory to God in the highest, and on earth peace, good will toward men.

And it came to pass, as the angels were gone away from them into heaven, the shepherds said one to another, Let us now go even unto Bethlehem, and see this thing which is come to pass, which the Lord hath made known unto us. And they came with haste, and found Mary, and Joseph, and the babe lying in a manger. And when they had seen it, they made known abroad the saying which was told them concerning this child. And all they that heard it wondered at those things which were told them by the shepherds. But Mary kept all these things, and pondered them in her heart.

Luke 2:1, 3-19

Merry Christmas

LOUISA MAY ALCOTT

Rosy feet upon the threshold,
Eager faces peeping through,
With the first red ray of sunshine,
Chanting cherubs come in view:
Mistletoe and gleaming holly,
Symbols of a blessed day,
In their chubby hands they carry,
Streaming all along the way.

Christmas, and I Remember

ROSE KORALEWSKY

'Tis Christmas Eve. Gay little candles burn,
Each haloed with a circlet of pure gold.
The tall tree glitters—red and green and blue;
Pink waxen angels' gauzy wings unfold.

We children all, mother and father too,
And still, adoring, in this mystic hour;
Round eyes of blue, small faces flushed with joy—
We feel, but do not understand, its power.

Then childish voices rise in "Silent Night"
While one by one the candles burn away;
The last flame dies, the sweet young voices fade;
But while I live, I keep this blessed day.

The Old-Fashioned Christmas Eve

MARJORIE HOLMES

Who remembers small-town Christmas Eves that were always celebrated with a pageant at the church and the snow that fell so softly as whole families headed toward this focal point?

Under the corner streetlamps the flakes spun and twinkled like fairies trying their wings. The whole earth wore a jeweled wrap, and your feet made little squeals on the hard-packed walks, like all the voices of excitement clamoring within.

The church smelled hot from the furnace. The spicy tang of the tree mingled with that of hymnals and galoshes and coffee brewing somewhere in huge granite pots.

Voices hummed, packages rattled, Sunday School teachers frantically assembled children in their proper rows. You swished your head, magnificently kinky from braids unbound, and imagined everybody was thinking how beautiful you were.

Shadows moved behind white sheets hung up for curtains. Garbed in bathrobes and turbaned in towels, your father and other men became strangers saying, "Let us go now even unto Bethlehem and see this thing which has come to pass." And the click and swish of the sheets being pulled. And at last the revelation: For there stood Joseph beside a manger with real straw. And Mary cradling a baby—sometimes a big doll, but once a real baby, the minister's new baby! You could hear it crowing and glimpse a moving hand. It lived! For a breathless, rapturous moment, the living, breathing Christ Child was right there in your midst.

Who remembers the programs with their songs and recitations? The desperately pounding heart as you swished forward in your crackling taffeta and new glory of curly hair. The horror of having to be prompted, the triumph of doing well.

And the smell of the tiny candles being lighted on the tree, twinkling stars to signal that something magic was about to happen. And the jangling of sleigh bells in the hall, and the superintendent asking, "What's this? Do I hear somebody?" And the wild and frenzied screaming, "Santa! Santa Claus!"

As you grew older, he began to look familiar, like Grandpa Griffith or old Mr. Samsel, or sometimes your dad. But no matter—when he patted you on the head or handed you a bag of hard candies he became the droll elf of the eternal fairy tale of North Pole and Make-Believe.

And the Ladies Aid served cookies and coffee. And parents visited, and children, mad with anticipation, begged to go home for the stockings yet to be hung. And at last you all poured out onto the steps that had been paved with ground diamonds.

"Good night, Merry Christmas, come to see us!" voices called as families set off along the cold, sparkling streets.

The snow had usually stopped by now. The night was still and clear. All the stars glittered. But there was always one bigger and brighter than the rest. A great gem that seemed to stand still as if to mark the mystery. You gazed at it in wonder all the way home.

A Christmas Carol

PHILLIPS BROOKS

Everywhere, everywhere, Christmas tonight!
Christmas in lands of the fir tree and pine,
Christmas in lands of the palm tree and vine,
Christmas where snow-peaks stand solemn and white,
Christmas where cornfields lie sunny and bright,
Everywhere, everywhere, Christmas tonight!

Christmas where children are hopeful and gay,
Christmas where old men are patient and gray,
Christmas where peace, like a dove in its flight,
Broods o'er brave men in the thick of the fight.
Everywhere, everywhere, Christmas tonight!

For the Christ Child who comes is the Master of all,
No palace too great and no cottage too small;
The angels who welcome Him sing from the height,
"In the City of David, a King in His might."
Everywhere, everywhere, Christmas tonight!

Then let every heart keep its Christmas within,
Christ's pity for sorrow, Christ's hatred for sin,
Christ's care for the weakest, Christ's courage for right,
Christ's dread of the darkness, Christ's love of the light,
Everywhere, everywhere, Christmas tonight!

So the stars of the midnight which compass us round
Shall see a strange glory, and hear a sweet sound,
And cry, "Look! the earth is aflame with delight,
O sons of the morning, rejoice at the sight."
Everywhere, everywhere, Christmas tonight!

Moravian Molasses Cookies

In a large bowl, place ⅓ cup melted vegetable shortening. Add 1 cup dark molasses and ½ cup firmly packed dark brown sugar; mix well. Set aside. In a small bowl, dissolve 1½ teaspoons baking soda in 2 tablespoons boiling water. Stir into molasses mixture; set aside. In a medium bowl, sift together 4 cups all-purpose flour, ½ teaspoon ground cinnamon, ½ teaspoon ground cloves, ½ teaspoon ground ginger, ½ teaspoon ground mace, and 1 teaspoon salt. Gradually add flour mixture and 1 teaspoon orange extract to molasses mixture; mix well, using your hands if necessary to work in all the flour. Wrap the dough in plastic wrap, refrigerate, and let set overnight or for several days.

Preheat oven to 350° F. Divide the dough into fifths, and, refrigerating the remainder, place one fifth of the dough on a floured surface. Lay a large piece of plastic wrap on top of the dough, and roll out as thin as possible.

Cut the dough with assorted, floured cookie cutters and place on a greased pan. Bake until very light brown, about 4 to 5 minutes, watching them very carefully. Allow the cookies to cool for 2 minutes, then remove to a wire rack. Continue rolling and baking the remaining dough as above. Store in air-tight tins. Makes 8 dozen cookies.

Mrs. Claus's Fudge

In a large Dutch oven, combine 4 cups granulated sugar, one 12-ounce can evaporated milk, and 1 cup butter. Place over medium heat and bring to a boil. Cook, stirring constantly, until mixture reaches the soft-ball stage (236° F). Remove from heat. Stir in one 12-ounce package chocolate chips, one 7-ounce jar marshmallow creme, 1 cup broken walnuts, and 1 teaspoon vanilla. Stir until chocolate is melted and mixture is smooth. Turn out into a buttered 13-by-9-by-2-inch baking pan. Score into squares while warm and top each square with a walnut half; chill until firm. Makes approximately 3½ pounds.

The Christmas Song

(CHESTNUTS ROASTING ON AN OPEN FIRE)

MUSIC AND LYRIC
BY MEL TORME AND ROBERT WELLS

Chest-nuts roast-ing on an o-pen fire, Jack Frost nip-ping at your nose,

Yule-tide car-ols be-ing sung by a choir And folks dressed up like Es-ki-mos. Ev-'ry-bod-y

knows a tur-key and some mis-tle-toe Help to make the sea-son bright.

Ti-ny tots with their eyes all a-glow Will find it hard to sleep to-

night. They know that San-ta's on his way; He's load-ed

A Perfect Day

WORDS AND MUSIC
BY CARRIE JACOBS-BOND

1. When you come to the end of a per-fect day, and you sit a-lone with your
2. Well,___ this is the end of a per-fect day, near the end of a jour - y

thoughts,___ While the chimes ring out with a car-ol gay, for the
too;___ But it leaves a thought that is big and strong, with a

joy that the day has brought; Do you think what the end of a
wish that is kind and true; For___ mem-'ry has paint-ed this

per-fect day can mean to a tired heart, when the
per-fect day with col-ors that nev - er fade, when and we

sun goes___ down with a flam-ing ray, and the dear friends___ have to part?
find at the end of a per-fect day the___ soul of a friend we've made.

Index

Photography Credits

C D E F G H I J
3 4 5 6 7 8 9 0

Cover: *Allies Day, May 1917* by Childe Hassam. Superstock. **Page 6**: The Tournament of Roses Parade 1938; courtesy of Pasadena Tournament of Roses. **9**: Crater Lake National Park, Oregon; Jon Gnass. **12**: Lancaster, Pennsylvania; Larry Lefever/Grant Heilman Photography, Inc. **14**: Little Redfish Lake Creek, Sawtooth National Forest, Idaho; Jon Gnass. **23**: Jerry Koser. **25**: *The New Skating Dance* by Lester Ralph. **26-27**: Sawtooth Range, Sawtooth National Forest, Idaho; Jon Gnass. **30**: Jerry Koser. **36**: Easter lilies with johnny-jump-ups, alyssum, iris, daffodils, and wisteria; Norman Poole. **38-39**: Rhododendrons and beargrass, Mt. Hood National Forest, Oregon; Steve Terrill Photography. **40**: Leslie Benson, artist. **42-43**: St. Simon's Island, Georgia; Superstock. **44**: Frances Hook, artist. **47**: Donald Mills, artist. **48**: South Harwich, Massachusetts; Dick Dietrich/Dietrich Photography. **52**: Dame's rocket and snow-in-summer; Larry Lefever/Grant Heilman Photography, Inc. **54-55**: Superstock. **58-59**: Azaleas and dogwoods, National Arboretum, Washington, D.C.; Ping Amranand/Superstock. **61**: *Mother and Child* by Mary Cassatt; Superstock. **63**: Courtesy of Ann Williams. **64**: Frances Hook, artist. **68**: Memorial Day, Arlington National Cemetery, Virginia; Peter Gridley/FPG International. **70-71**: Bluebonnets and Indian paintbrush, Kingsland, Texas; Josiah Davidson Scenic Photography. **72**: Ralph Morang/New England Stock Photo. **77**: Poppies; Superstock. **85**: Beaver Pond, New Boston, New Hampshire; Alan Briere/Superstock. **89**: John Walter, artist. **90-91**: Wild balsamroot on Hood River Mountain, Oregon; Steve Terrill Photography. **98-99**: Fourth of July fireworks, Boston, Massachusetts; Thayer Syme/FPG International. **100**: Courtesy of the United States Marine Corps Band. **102-103**: Grand Teton National Park, Wyoming; Chad Ehlers/International Stock. **104**: Mailbox with American flag, Acton, Massachusetts; John Wells/New England Stock Photo. **106-107**: Superstock. **108**: The flag of the United States that flew over Fort McHenry in 1814 and inspired Francis Scott Key to write "The Star Spangled Banner," Armed Forces History Division, Museum of American History, Smithsonian Institution. **112**: Dexter Mill, Sandwich, Cape Cod, Massachusetts; Superstock. **114-115**: Wychmere Boat Harbor, Cape Cod, Massachusetts; J. Blank/H. Armstrong Roberts. **116**: Morristown National Historical Park, New Jersey; Jeff Gnass Photography. **118-119**: *Snap the Whip* by Winslow Homer, Butler Institute of Art; Superstock. **120**: Superstock. **128**: Plimoth Plantation, Plymouth, Massachusetts; Ted Curtin/Plimoth Plantation, Inc. **130-131**: *The Embarcation of the Pilgrims* by Robert W. Weir; Superstock. **132**: Mt. Shuksan, Washington; D. Carriere/H. Armstrong Roberts. **135**: *American Homestead Autumn* by Currier & Ives. **136-137**: New Hampshire; Superstock. **139**: Superstock. **140**: Jerry Koser. **144**: Boonton, New Jersey; Superstock. **147**: George Hinke. **148**: Larry Lefever/Grant Heilman Photography, Inc. **151**: Frances Hook, artist. **152**: Jessie Walker Associates. **155**: Brookline, Massachusetts; Dianne Dietrich Leis. **158**: Virginia; Superstock.

Details of the following Norman Rockwell illustrations were printed by permission of the Norman Rockwell Family Trust. Copyright © 1996 the Norman Rockwell Family Trust: **Page 5**: *Clock Repairman*, cover of *The Saturday Evening Post*, November 3, 1945. **19**: *Cupid's Visit*, cover of *The Saturday Evening Post*, April 5, 1924. **35**: *The Choir Boy*, cover of *The Saturday Evening Post*, April 17, 1954. **51**: *A Mother's Love*, cover of *The Literary Digest*, January 29, 1921. Courtesy of the Norman Rockwell Museum at Stockbridge. **67**: *A Salute to the Colors*, cover of *The Saturday Evening Post*, May 12, 1917. **75**: *The Trumpeter*, cover of *The Saturday Evening Post*, November 18, 1950. **81**: *The Parade*, cover of *The Literary Digest*, May 28, 1921. **95**: *Mending the Flag*, cover of *The Literary Digest*, May 27, 1922. Courtesy of the Norman Rockwell Museum at Stockbridge. **111**: *Home from Vacation*, cover of *The Saturday Evening Post*, September 13, 1930. **127**: *Home for Thanksgiving*, cover of *The Saturday Evening Post*, November 24, 1945. **143**: *Merry Christmas*, cover of *The Saturday Evening Post*, December 8, 1928.